The (
Healing Wells
of the Western Isles

The Chapels *and* Healing Wells *of the* Western Isles

Finlay MacLeod

Registered Charity SC047866

'The Chapels In The Western Isles' first published in Scotland in 1997 by Acair Ltd

'The Healing Wells of the Western Isles' first published in Scotland in 2000 by Acair Ltd.

This combined edition published in 2018 by Acair, An Tosgan, Seaforth Road, Stornoway, Isle of Lewis, Scotland HS1 2SD

www.acairbooks.com
info@acairbooks.com

The cover and interior design of this edition by Joan MacRae-Smith for Acair

A CIP catalogue record for this title is available from the British Library

Printed by Hussar Books, Poland.

ISBN 978-1-78907-001-9

Contents

The **Chapels**

Starting off... 7

    Lewis 15

    Outer Islands 40

    Harris 46

    North Uist 56

    Benbecula 67

    South Uist 71

    Barra 79

    The Bishops's Isles 83

Bibliography 87

The **Healing Wells**

Introduction 94

The Well 104

    Lewis 107

    Harris 122

    North Uist 127

    Benbecula 133

    South Uist 135

    Barra 140

    St. Kilda 148

Bibliography 153

The
Chapels

illustrations
Christine Campbell

STARTING OFF

This book aims to be a guide for those who are out and about in the Western Isles and who are seeking to find out more about the many interesting features here – in this case the range of chapel sites situated throughout the Islands. The location of the sites is given and reference is made to the writings of earlier visitors to the sites.

The book does not aim to provide a detailed description of the buildings but is intended more as an introductory text to encourage younger people to take an active interest in the Hebridean environment and culture. The book was published earlier in Gaelic as a text for secondary school students. It could just as easily be a book about island wells, stills, corn mills, kilns, early schools, etc: the particular topic serves mainly to encourage people to go out into the countryside to enjoy its varied texture.

For those wishing to go on to learn more about the historical framework within which the chapels may be placed, they could begin with the writings of Ian B. Cowan and particularly his book, 'The Parishes of Medieval Scotland'

(1967), and his seminal paper, 'The Development of the Parochial System in Medieval Scotland'. Cowan writes that the basic unit in the organisation of the Medieval Church in Scotland was the parish. The pattern of parishes established by the twelfth century lasted until the Reformation. The chapels of the Western Isles are described in the present book according to the various parishes within the diocese which was named 'Sodor'.

On the ground, one imagines the visitor or student in the vicinity of one of the sites, and being approached by a local resident who is working on his croft on the machair:

"That is Teampall Eòin ahead of you," ventures the crofter. "St. John's Chapel."

"I thought it was," says the seeker, writing the name in his notebook.

He writes: "Teampall Eòin. St. John's Chapel. NB 288488".

"It is also called Cill Sgàire," ventures the crofter.

"How very unusual," the visitor.

"Very unusual," the crofter. "Viking influence."

The crofter turns round and points: "There used to be a special well along there. Called Fuaran Buaile Dhòmhnaill. But it was destroyed by a digger a few years ago."

"The Well on Donald's Enclosure?" translates the visitor.

"The Well on Donald's Enclosure," reassures the crofter. "Maybe it was used by the priests from the Chapel."

"How old is the Chapel?" asks the visitor.

The crofter laughs. "No idea, No idea whatsoever. Only the ruined site and its name remain."

"Surprising that," observes the visitor.

"Surprising, indeed," muses the crofter.

The names of most of the chapels have survived and they too are included in this book. In a few instances the actual site cannot be located accurately although the name survives. St. Clement's in Ness in Lewis is one such example. The names reflect the changes that occurred within the early Church in the Gaelic areas; the earlier phase of naming is seen in the chapels dedicated to Saints such as Ronan, Donan, Moluidh and Columba, and the later influence of the centralist Church is seen in names such as St. Peter's, St. John's and St. Mary's. These names are frequently used for the burial grounds where chapels are located, as well as for nearby physical features such as streams or hills, and also for wells which are sometimes found close to the chapels.

Tradition has retained scant knowledge of the priests who attended the chapels or how the chapels themselves were integrated into the everyday communities of the times. The chapels tend to be fairly small and are situated usually near the shore, where the older townships were located. It is intriguing to observe where each of the many sites is located throughout the islands: it is sometimes as puzzling to understand why there isn't a site in a given township as it is to understand why others are situated where they are.

In terms of access, it is easier to walk round these sites in winter or early in spring when they are clear of nettles and other growth. Not infrequently the sites are in old and sometimes abandoned burial grounds and very few of them have been cared for in any way. Most of them are fairly dilapidated and only a small number have been renovated.

In a way, it is surprising how the chapels have survived, unattended but undamaged during the islands' numerous church vicissitudes. But they survive in silence; with little interest in them and little done to bring them to the attention of the islands' young or to revive them in any form of art or festival.

One's quest could readily begin with the site nearest to home.

You will note whether or not it is set in an old burial-ground.

You will note whether or not it is close to an old, pre-crofting settlement.

You will note whether or not there is a special, named well nearby.

There may be someone living in the village who will know something about the site, including its name or any related tradition.

Each Local History Society is likely to have some basic information about the sites in the locality.

The local library will direct you to some books which include accounts written by visitors in earlier years.

The archaeological work on the chapel sites has been very patchy and little progress has been made since the comprehensive 1928 ancient monuments survey. Most of the buildings are beautifully small, in rectangular form. Some of the smaller ones have a nave and chancel but these are few and far between. In many cases the sites have become seriously denuded with only the base outline of the walls remaining; in some cases only a green knoll marks the site. The buildings that have been renovated most extensively include Tùr Mòr Chiamain/St. Clement's, Rodil, Teampall Mholuidh, Ness, the church on Ensay, and Cille Bharra in Barra. The largest of the ruined sites are at Howmore in South Uist, Carinish in North Uist, and Eye in Lewis.

These largely abandoned sites together build up a most intriguing network of locations throughout the length of the Western Isles; the fact that they still exist is surprising in itself, and the fact that they form such an unspoken part of the landscape and the history of the place contrasts with the more strident forms of belief which arrived in the islands during subsequent centuries.

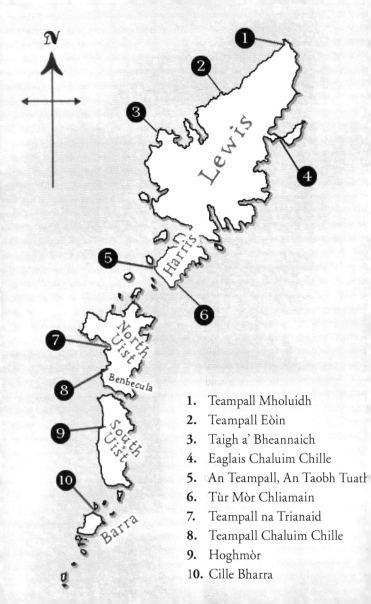

1. Teampall Mholuidh
2. Teampall Eòin
3. Taigh a' Bheannaich
4. Eaglais Chaluim Chille
5. An Teampall, An Taobh Tuath
6. Tùr Mòr Chliamain
7. Teampall na Trianaid
8. Teampall Chaluim Chille
9. Hoghmòr
10. Cille Bharra

LEWIS

Teampall Rònain

NB 524654

This site is located on a hillock approximately a mile south-east of the Butt of Lewis lighthouse. It is among the Eoropie crofts, and only the foundations remain. It was originally about 24 feet long and 18 feet wide. There is no evidence of a graveyard close to it. Hardly anyone visits this site now although it is quite accessible.

Folklore relates that this chapel was associated with St. Ronan and the story is told of how he left Eoropie and how he got to North Rona on the back of a large whale. (See Carmina Gadelica, 1, 1972, 126-7; Robson, 1991, 2-6 and 165).

St. Ronan's Well is by the main road, but when the road was widened the well was badly affected. Often chapels and wells were located close to one another.

Teampall Mholuidh

Teampall Mholuidh NB 519652

This is a famous chapel and you can see why.

It is old and imposing and a lot has been written and told about it. It is located in Eoropie and many people visit it because it is accessible to the main road by a footpath.

According to historians such as W.C. Mackenzie (1903/1932) it was once called 'Teampall Mòr' by the inhabitants. There is no sign of a graveyard close by although there may well have been one.

It is almost 45 feet long and 18 feet wide with tall limestone walls and attractive windows. To the north a small room is attached and a little chapel is similarly attached to the south side. It was re-roofed in 1912 and it is still used for worship. The chapel features highly in oral tradition as follows:

- how the people knelt as soon as they could see the chapel, although they may be miles from it.
- how they believed that a person suffering from mental illness could be restored to health by sleeping there for one night, tied to the altar.
- how they walked clockwise around it.
- how they placed a piece of wood in similar shape to the affected part of the body (i.e. hand or foot) to enable actual healing to take place.
- how they used water from St. Ronan's Well nearby.
- how they held their Hallowe'en feasts there before going out to eat and dance and offer a cup of ale to the god Seònaidh on a nearby beach. (See Martin, 1934, 107-108; Pochin Mould, 1953, 175-178).

Teampall Thòmais   NB 507641

All that remains on this site is a few stones from one of
the walls. It is at the top of a grassy hill by the shore on
Swainbost machair, and there is a hollow within the site. It
is approximately 100 yards from St. Peter's Chapel and there
is no sign of gravestones in close proximity. According to
tradition its stones were used to build St. Peter's.

Teampall Pheadair   NB 508637

This site is located in the old graveyard in Swainbost and
is the second largest chapel in Lewis. The largest is St.
Columba's at Eye.

St. Peter's is over 60 feet long, but the only remaining part
is the southernmost end which has an attractive window.

It is in a beautiful location, in the western spot of the
graveyard with the Swainbost river close by.

Between it and the shore is a place called 'Na h-Annaidean'
and 'Cnoc an Annaid'. 'Annaid' is an ancient name for a
church location. This name also is found in Shader, close to
St. Peter's Chapel, and on Killegray in the Sound of Harris,
and in Eilean Garbh in the Shiants.

Teampall Chliamain

NB 4962

Located in North Dell, there is no sign of this site now, nor much account of it in oral tradition. Martin Martin calls it, 'St. Clemen in Dell'.

The Ordnance Survey Book (ONB) writes, "Dun Cleamon…Its site is now ploughed over. A polished stone was found near site of dun (1890). Site is not known locally."

Teampall nan Crò Naomh

NB 433593

This chapel is on South Galson machair, down by the shore. Martin Martin refers to it as 'Holy-Cross church in Galan'.

It is important because Daniel made a painting of it in 1819 when it was mainly intact although without a roof. The gables have since collapsed and sand covers much of the site.

There are three windows in the east wall and there are holes in the inside of the walls.

According to tradition it was once thatched with heather.

Teampall Bhrìghid

NB 410573

This chapel is situated in Melbost; with a few gravestones round about it. All that remains is the raised site and a few stones. Many of the stones have been removed, or have disappeared into the ground.

St. Brighid's Well is close by.

According to tradition Swain, a Norse king, is buried here with his crown and his sword.

Teampall Pheadair

This chapel is situated on a green sward above Mol Eire in Shader. A grassy knoll can still be seen on the site with a small amount of wall still showing. It was over 33 feet long and apparently it comprised two rooms; these were the nave and chancel.

Beside the chapel is Creag Gille Phàdraig. Clach an t-Sagairt could at one time be seen by the shore until it was eroded by the force of the sea some years back.

St. Andrew's Well, mentioned by Martin Martin, can be found east of the chapel, and Tobair Mhoire is slightly to the south of it.

Rubha na h-Annaid lies 100 yards east of the chapel and the large stones which are called Clachan na h-Annaid are about 100 yards south of Rubha na h-Annaid near St. Andrew's Well.

Teampall Mhoire

This chapel was situated in Barvas cemetery but it is now engulfed by sand.

We know that it was there in the 15th century because a letter from the Pope in Rome, dated 27 May 1403, states, "To all the Christian faithful – Indult granting an indulgence to visitors to the church of St. Mary in Barwas in the isle of Lewis, diocese of Sodor, on certain feast days and those who contribute to its reparation", as if people could not normally use it, and it also suggests that it was even then being repaired.

According to Dean Monro (1549) this chapel was one of 4 parish churches in Lewis: the others were in Ness, in Uig and in Point (Cowan, 1967).

In his book, A Tour of the Hebrides (1803) James Hogg writes "On the top of one of these hills is situated St. Mary's chapel, an ancient place of Popish worship. It had formerly been on the very summit of the eminence, but the sand is now heaped up to such a height as to be on a level with the gables. Yet the eddying winds have still kept it nearly clear, so that it appears as a building wholly sunk underground. The baptismal font is still standing in a place in the wall prepared for it." (III).

In 1861 T.S. Muir wrote, "The church – St. Mary – is said to be existing under the sand, which has also completely overwhelmed the ancient graveyard." (186).

Teampall Eòin

This chapel is known by two names: St. John's Chapel and Cill Sgàire. 'Cill' is Celtic, and Sgàire is a personal Norse name still found in Lewis: St. John's Chapel is the newer and more Roman name.

This is an attractive building and it is better preserved than many other chapels. It can be found in the old Bragar graveyard.

It is approximately 29 feet long and has two rooms; the nave and chancel. Experts are of the opinion that it was built in the 15th century.

At one time there was a special spring close by called Fuaran Buaile Dhòmhnaill but a JCB destroyed it some years back. The remains of an old village can be seen adjacent to the graveyard and a kitchen midden can be seen above the shore line. An underground channel was discovered between that spot and the graveyard itself a few years back.

Teampall Eòin

Teampall Dail Mòr   NB 218448

This building was knocked down sometime after 1914 and the stones were used to build the house next door. T.S. Muir wrote in 1885, "At Dailmor…the remains of an apparently not very old chapel, 60 feet in length." (41-2). In the Royal Commission (1928) it is written that they visited it in 1914: "This church… is of comparatively recent date. It is an ordinary oblong structure with no features of interest." (1).

There is no sign of it nowadays and even its name is unknown. There was no graveyard near it. Martin Martin does not mention it; maybe it had not been built when he visited.

Between the two wars visitors came to seek it out, but the man next door told them, "Gone… Gone…" Gone indeed.

Teampall Chiarain   NB 187424

This chapel was situated in Carloway, above Laimsiadair, but cannot now be seen. Historic references tell us that those who were ill were brought to this chapel and that they were walked clockwise round the building, and made to sleep the night inside. They believed that this would cure the afflicted person.

Close by was a cairn at the top of a steep path, called 'Slighe Chiarain'; the cairn was known as 'Beannachadh Ciaraig' (NB 190424). Passers-by would place a stone on the cairn; the site can still be seen.

At the end of Slighe Chiarain and slightly to the north is Fuaran Chiarain. Martin Martin mentions this spring and says that water from it could not successfully wash linen.

Teampall Mhìcheil NB 195417

This chapel was in Kirvick in Carloway but only the base foundation exists today. It is in an old cemetery.

T.S. Muir wrote in 1861, "Hardly anything of it remains, and the burying-ground is now but rarely used." (186). The Ordnance Survey map of 1850 refers to the village beside the graveyard as 'Baile an Teampaill'.

Teampall Dhonain NB 152406

This site can be found at the south end of Tràigh an Teampaill in Little Bernera. It is also called the Teampall Iosal. Only the shape remains, covered in grass and sand. Close by are Rubha Phapanais and Cnoc an t-Sagairt.

In 1861 T.S. Muir wrote, "Another chapel – St. Donnan – was standing not many years since lower down on a snout of land close to the beach, but no traces of it are now extant." (177).

The lovely tale is told of Swain the Norse king, and how he took Gealchos, daughter of the young priest with him from Tràigh an Teampaill to Norway. But her heart broke mourning for Little Bernera and he brought her back. Her song is still known. (see D. Dòmhnallach, 1967, 228-234).

Teampall Mhìcheil   NB 151406

This site is also on Little Bernera, and nothing is left save the rise of the walls. It is beside the burial aisle of John Macdonald which is built similar to an old chapel.

T.S. Muir writes in 1861, "Directly above a smaller tràigh (Tràigh an Teampaill) on the eastern side of the island, there is an open burying-ground, containing a few bare slabs of ancient type, and the groundwork of St. Michael's chapel occupying the top of a rock." (177). Muir stayed with John Macdonald at Taigh a' Chaolais at the time.

A short distance from Little Bernera is Eilean Fir Chrothair (NB 139418) which has stone beehive dwellings, with one of them still almost intact. The local people call it 'Am Beannachadh' (The Blessing Place). Small buildings similar to these can be seen on remote islands in different places throughout the islands; they could have been prayer houses used by anchorites.

Teampall Chirceboist   NB 191346

In the village of Kirkibost in Bernera can be found the site of an old chapel. Locals believe that this is the chapel referred to in Martin Martin's book as 'St. Macrel'. Origines (1857) refers to it as 'Saint Macra the Virgin'.

An old graveyard is close to the chapel and another site called, 'An Taigh Sgoile'. The chapel site is near Loch Mharcoil, and maybe it was called 'Teampall Mharcoil'.

Macaulay (c1984) says that there is a Teampall Chaluim Chille in Great Bernera but, if there is, no-one knows where.

Teampall Pheadair NB 105376

Situated on the lovely island of Pabbay close to Valtos, Uig, and above Tràigh na Cille, this chapel has all but disappeared. The lower walls remain, with the sill of one window to the west. It looks as if a chancel was situated at the east end.

"The church on Pabay More in Loch Roag, Lewis, bears a dedication to St. Peter. This marks the grafting of the new style on the old. After the synod of Whitby (664) the Celtic Church gradually conformed to Roman usages, including that of dedications. How soon or how late this change would affect the Isles is impossible to say." (Royal Commission, 1928, xlvii).

T.S. Muir wrote in 1861, "Made up of a smooth sandy beach, rock, and flowery pasture, Eilean Pabba had much of that peculiar sweetness of aspect which somehow invariably belongs to islands of the name... The scant remains of St. Peter's chapel – a rude and narrow oblong some eight-and-twenty feet in length in the middle of a nearly obliterated burying-ground – being the only object of interest." (177).

Two interesting lobster ponds can be found at the north end of the island.

Teampall Bhaltois   NB 089367

This chapel is in the Valtos graveyard above Cliff Beach.

T.S. Muir writes in 1885, "… the foundations of a chapel, internally 18 feet in length." (41). Its name is unknown. To this day a knoll in the graveyard is referred to as 'An Teampall', and the surrounding area is called 'Leathad an Teampaill'.

A raised grassy spot about a mile south-east of this site is called 'An Teampall' (NB 098363). It is close to the northwest end of Tràigh na Beirghe.

Taigh a' Bheannaich   NB 038378

About a mile south west of Gallan Head in Uig this site is close to the shore, and to a headland called 'Am Beannachadh' (The Blessing Place), close to Loch a' Bheannaich. Tobair a' Bheannaich is about 32 yards south west of the chapel.

D. Macdonald (1967) also mentions. 'Geò a' Bheannaich' and 'Faing a' Bheannaich'.

T.S. Muir writing in 1861 says, "On Gallon Head – Tigh Beannaichte (Blessed House), or Tigh Beannachadh (Blessing House), as it is locally called – is, except that the roof is wanting, nearly entire. The internal dimensions are 18ft. 2in., by 10ft. 4in. From the appearance of the masonry, which is without lime, and other peculiar features, it would seem a very old building." (174).

Taigh a' Bheannaich

An Teampall, Baile na Cille

This chapel was situated in the graveyard at Baile na Cille, and is referred to by Martin Martin as 'St. Christopher's'. The writer I.N. MacLeòid was of the opinion that it was called Cille Chrìosd.

The Royal Commission (1928) says, "There is an old kirkyard, beside the highest part of which stood an old church built in 1724. The site was occupied by an earlier church, Capail Mor ("Big Chapel"), the foundations of which are said to be traceable in spring. To the south of it is the site of Capail Beg ("Little Chapel"), possibly a still earlier church." (18).

It is strange that oral tradition does not provide more information on these chapels. Maybe this is as a consequence of the fact that chapels were being built and knocked down round about Baile na Cille.

An Teampall, Mealasta

Mealista is the most westerly village in Uig.

T.S. Muir states in 1885, "At Mealastadh, on its south-west side, are traces of a small building called Taigh nan Cailleachan Dubha, House of the Black Old Women (Nuns); and in an open, grassy, and flowery burial-ground, the foundations of a chapel, internally about 19 feet in length, and a rudely-formed font of elleptical shape." (40).

And the Royal Commission (1928) says, "About 200 yards west of Mealista farmhouse, on a rocky point on the south of the promontary Rudh' an Teampaill, rising only

20 feet above high-water mark, are the foundations of the church, measuring externally 25 feet in length and 15 feet 8 inches in breadth, with the wall 2 feet 8 inches thick and oriented south of east and north of west. Between the church and the sea is a small burying ground. (18).

"At Mealista, Uig, there was a shrine to St Catan (see Teampall na h-Aoidh), near which has been found the remains of a nunnery, locally known as the 'house of the black old women'." (W.C. Mackenzie, 1903, 518).

Strangely there is no reference in oral tradition to Taigh nan Cailleachan Dubha – only the name and location. In Lewis one often spoke of the distance along the west coast by saying, "From the House of the Black Women in Uig to Taigh Mholuidh in Eoropie."

Teampall Chaluim Chille   NB 386211

St Columba's Isle in Loch Erisort is well known in Lewis history as a fertile, beautiful and peaceful spot. St. Columba's chapel is situated in the graveyard on that island.

"The church is oblong on plan and measures internally 29 feet 6 inches by 13 feet 3 inches, the walls still standing to an average of 6 feet and measuring 2 feet 6 inches thick." (Royal Commission, 1928, 11).

One of Derick Thomson's poems bemoans how the place has changed: "Eilean Chaluim Chille, an Loch Eireasort, Leòdhas' (1967).

An Teampall, Rànais   NB 399248

There is a site in Ranish called Cnoc an Teampaill where the remains of an old graveyard are still evident and the lower part of the chapel walls.

It was approximately 20 feet long by 12 feet wide. Nowadays no-one can tell of its history although the name of the area is still used. We have no knowledge of the name of the chapel.

An Teampall, Cathanais   NB 389234

Martin Martin refers to this chapel as St. Pharaer in Kaeness. Cathanais is located in Suardail in Loch Liurbost, but the remains of the chapel are no longer visible. At one time there was a farm and a township here. Neither is it known who St. Pharaer was, and there is no reference to such a saint anywhere else. Martin Martin did not elaborate, but merely referred to him as St. Pharaer in Kaeness. Some do not accept that this was the chapel to which Martin referred; and that he might really have meant the Ranish chapel.

Teampall Leannain

This chapel was situated in central Stornoway, although all that now remains is the name and the church bell. Martin Martin referred to it as "'St. Lennan in Sternvay'. It was situated in a graveyard on North Beach close to where the Royal Bank of Scotland and the Sailors' Home are at present. One of the chapel doors was later used as the outside door of a shoemaker's shop in the town. W.C. Mackenzie (1919) states, "St. Lennan was built by the 1st Earl of Seaforth who died in 1633 – the pre-Reformation church having fallen into disrepair."

Macaulay (c1984) says, "The pre-Reformation church at Stornoway was dedicated to St. Adamnan." (42). But he does not disclose the source of his information.

An account written by Lord Teignmouth in 1829 tells of how the tide was intruding into the graveyard and exposing the remains. It is also related that the building was in danger of falling and that it was one Dòmhnall Ceàrd who eventually demolished it for the reward of one and a half bolls of meal. "Oh, Donald Ceàrd of the boll and a half meal. Had you been given the other half you would have had even the Pope's own image on the ground." (D. Macdonald, 1967, 297).

The bell from this chapel is still used in St. Peter's in Stornoway.

Martin Martin also mentions 'Stornvay Church' but there is no information available concerning this church.

Eaglais Chaluim Chille

Eaglais Chaluim Chille NB 485323

Undoubtedly this church was one of the best known in the islands, and it was the foremost Lewis church at one time. It is situated at Eye and was built by one of the MacLeod chiefs and dedicated to St. Catan. "As Ui was the 'Iona' of Sìol Thorquil, so was Rodil (Tùr Chliamain) the 'Iona' of Sìol Thormod." (W.C. MacKenzie, 1903, 519).

It is a large building but it is neglected and much in need of repair. Each wall and gable is intact and it is a great pity that no one takes responsibility for it. It is situated in the old Eye Churchyard in Aignish by the shore and many MacLeod chiefs are buried there, and grave slabs can be seen there. Martin Martin refers to it as 'St. Colum in Eye'.

W.C. MacKenzie (1919) states that according to tradition there had been a cell on this site dedicated to St. Catan (6th and 7th century) and a holy house. Much has been written about St. Columba's Church as it is so well known. (see T.S. Muir, 1861, 167; T.S. Muir, 1885, 39-40; Royal Commission, 1928, 12-14; D. MacDonald, 1967, 264-266; Barber, 1987; Bill Lawson, 1991).

Teampall Chùistein

This chapel was situated in Garrabost in Point. Martin Martin refers to it as 'St. Cuthcon'. He also says, "The well at St. Cowsten's Church never boils any kind of meat, though it be kept on fire a whole day." (90).

Some think that it was really St. Constantine's, but this may not be so.

T.S. Muir (1861) states, "Of St. Cowstan's chapel, once in Garrabost… nothing now remains, the site having sometime been ploughed and put under crop; but the holy well, still remembered as that consecrated by the patron saint, and regarded the sweetest water in the place, still trickles down its steep declivity to the shore." (167).

The Ordnance Survey Book (ONB) states the following about the chapel, "It is situated on a piece of sloping ground on the north of and adjacent to Allt Buaile Eòin about 4 chains west of Tobar an Leothaid. Around 1808 the walls were completely levelled for building the walls of huts etc. There is no sign of it today. St. Cowstan's Well: tradition is that all manners of diseases used to be cured by placing the patient under the cliff when the water fell to the shore." (ONB, Lewis, 21, 1848).

Teampall Rubha Chirc   NB 507292

Neither Martin Martin nor T.S. Muir refer to this chapel. But the site is referred to on the first Ordnance Survey map c1850. There is no information about its dedication.

The Royal Commission (1928) says, "About 5/8 mile east of Chicken Head, in a small rivulet near the edge of a cliff which rises more than 100 feet out of the sea, are the foundations of a stone and mud building measuring about 18 feet in length and 15 feet in breadth, oriented west-north-west and east-south-east." (14).

Teampall Aulaidh   NB 491415

Martin Martin refers to this chapel as 'St. Aula in Grease'. The Royal Commission (1928) states, "St. Aulay (Olaf) at Gress, Lewis, is the only Norse saint among the dedications." (xclvi). (Cill Sgàire is the original name for Teampall Eòin in Bragar). The walls and gables of this chapel are still intact, but a shelter has been built at one end of it.

T.S. Muir (1861) states, "Col and Gress, lying some few miles north of Stornoway, are both sweet spots. At the latter is the church of St. Aula, standing in an open though cleanly burying-ground a little way up from the shore: it is a very small building, the internal length being barely 19 feet, the walls nearly entire, but without any peculiar features." (168).

Above the main door is written '1681 1B MK' – as if it had been repaired that year.

Teampall Mhìcheil NB 544481

This chapel was in North Tolsta, in Cladh Mhìcheil above the Tràigh Mhòr. Martin Martin refers to it as 'St. Michael in Tollasta'.

T.S. Muir (1885) says, "At Tolsta… is the burying-ground of St. Michael, on a grassy slope overlooking a long stretch of smooth sandy shore, but in it are no traces of the church under the dedication mentioned by Martin." (43-44).

Donald Macdonald from Tolsta wrote a book about the village in 1984: "There is now no trace of the old chapel, dedicated to St. Michael, the Celtic Neptune, probably similar to St. Olaf's in Gress, which stood about fifty yards up from the north east corner (of the graveyard), where its large foundation stones can still be found. In 1820 part of its walls were still standing and ponies used to shelter here on cold winter nights." (55).

The stream which runs through the village of Tolsta is called Allt Chaluim Chille.

Teampall Chaluim Chille

Martin Martin refers to this chapel as 'St. Collum in Garien'.

No one knows of this location. Some people believe it was in Garry.

It is not known whether it had any links with Allt Chaluim Chille in Tolsta.

The Origines (1851) map places it at Cnoc a' Ghearraidh Ghuirm in Coll, but we cannot be certain that this is correct.

Dun Othail and An Luchraban

(NB 543515) (NB 511661)

These are two isolated sites and some written accounts refer to them as having been chapels, or prayer house, as could have been in Eilean Fir Chrothair.

T.S. Muir (1861) states, "At Dun Othail, in a shelf down in the face of the precipice, is an architectural remain – of an early chapel, probably." (168). But there are sites on places such as Dùn Filiscleitir, Dùn Eòradail and Dùn Eistean along this coast, and they have never been referred to as sites of chapels.

Dean Monro (1549) says of the Luchraban, "At the northern poynt of Lewis there is a little ile, callit the Pigmies ile, with ane little kirk in it of ther awn handey wark." (82-83).

An anonymous account written between 1577 and 1599 states, "In this (Pygmies) Isle thair is ane little Cove biggit in form of ane kirk, and callit the Pygmies Kirk." Blaeu's map (1654) also shows it as a chapel and calls the island 'Ylen Dunibeg' (Island of the little people).

OUTER ISLANDS

*These are Rona and Sulaisgeir; the Shiants;
the Flannan Isles; and St. Kilda.*

Rona

HW 809323

Rona is situated about 50 miles north-east of Ness in Lewis; it is close to Sulasgeir, and they are separated by Caolas Rònaigh – 10 miles wide.

To this day, in Ness, oral tradition relates how St. Ronan fled from Ness to Rona to get peace and quiet, and how he chased the wild things out to sea when he arrived on Rona.

There is a wonderful folktale describing how a huge animal not unlike a whale carried him to Rona on its back. The animal was called a cianaran-crò. (see Carmichael, 1, 126-127; 2, 348; 6, 115-116).

St. Ronan's cell is one of the most important of its kind in Europe. Because the island is so inaccessible the cell walls are still intact. Round about the 12th century a chapel was attached to the cell, and the walls of that chapel can still be seen although they have fallen in part. Writers have related many stories about the Rona people, their customs and their beliefs. It is a most interesting island in every respect. (see Monro, 1549/1961, 88; Martin, 100-104, Morrison (Indweller) c1683/1989, 27; T.S. Muir, 1885, 90-96; Royal Commission, 1928,3-4; Fraser Darling, 1939; Robson, 1991, 6-9).

There is a collection of stones close to Cill Rònain and maybe this is Teampall Mhionagain, although one cannot be entirely sure. T.S. Muir (1886) mentions that 'Teampall nam Manach' was in this locality.

There were beautiful stone crosses in the graveyard close to the Cell; the most singular one is now with Comann Eachdraidh Nis, as is a round stone dug up by Fraser Darling near the altar in St. Ronan's Cell.

Sùlaisgeir HW 621307

Tradition has it that Rònan's sister – Brianuilt – fled from Rona to Sùlasgeir. There can still be seen there a large stone bench which is called 'Suide Bhrianuilt'.

There is also a stone building there like a large beehive dwelling. Unfortunately, its roof collapsed a few years ago.

T.S. Muir (1886) states, "On a small semi-insulated spot, closely surrounded by rocks, marked Sgeir an Teampaill in the Ordnance map, there is a low rugged building with rounded corners and a curved roof, called Tigh Beanaichte (Blessed House), internally 14 feet long, and 8 feet wide in the middle, and 6 feet 4 inches at the ends." (98).

THE SHIANTS

These islands are about 4 miles east of Park, Lewis.
There are three islands: Garbh Eilean;
Eilean an Taighe and Eilean Mhuire.
They are also known as na h-Eileanan Mòra.

Teampall Mhuire   NG 431986

Teampall Mhuire was situated on Eilean Mhuire but even
the walls are now underground. Apparently it had strong
limestone walls, and was situated in the graveyard. Martin
Martin says, "Island-More hath a chapel in it dedicated to
the Virgin Mary." (105).

Eilean Taighe   NG 419972

T.S. Muir writing in 1885 said, "On the west side… On
this level space there are traces of a burying-ground, and
the foundation of what seems to have been a chapel of small
size." (56). This is the only known reference to it.

Eilean Garbh   NG 412983

Airighean na h-Annaid is referred to as a placename on this
island. But there is no information about there having been
a chapel.

THE FLANNAN ISLES

The Flannan Isles   NB 727469

These islands are 20 miles west of Lewis. They comprise 3 groups of islands, two of which were inhabited: Eilean Mòr and Eilean Taigh. The famous lighthouse and the chapel are situated on Eilean Mòr. This lovely little chapel is still intact. T.S. Muir reports that it was called 'Teampall Beannachadh' (Chapel of Blessings) and there is a spot close to the chapel called 'Am Beannachadh'.

Martin Martin says, "The biggest of these islands is called Island-More; it has the ruins of a chapel dedicated to St. Flannan, from whom the island derives its name. When they (Lewis seabird-hunters) are come to within about 20 paces of the alter, they all strip themselves of their upper garments at once… the first day they say the first prayer, advancing towards the chapel upon their knees; the second prayer is said as they go round the chapell; the third is said hard by or at the chapel." (98).

The Royal Commission (1928) says, "On Eilean Mòr… stand the remains of a tiny chapel. Single chambered and rectangular on plan, it measures only 5 by 7¾ feet within walls 26 to 30 inches in thickness. The roof, which had fallen, had been roughly rebuilt. It was built of thin flat slabs… The masonry of the chapel is dry-built and is rude in character, giving no clue to the date of the structure." (30).

ST. KILDA

St. Kilda

Many books have been written about St. Kilda and this trend will probably continue – although no St. Kildans have lived there for 60 years.

Martin Martin says, "There are three chappels on the isle, each of them with one end towards the east, the other towards the west; the alter always placed at the east end; the first of these is called Christ Chappel, near the village; it is covered and thatched after the same manner with their houses... The second of these chappels bears the name of St. Columba, the third of St. Brianan; both built after the manner of Christ's chappel; having churchyards belonging to them, and they are a quarter of a mile distant betwixt each chappel." (443, 445).

In 1764 Macaulay says: "A temple has been dedicated to that illustrious Abbot there, which in the language of the place is called Columbcille to this day: it lies on the west side of the village, and has neither alter, cross or cell within its precincts...

"The largest church on St. Kilda is dedicated to Christ, and is called his temple. It was built of stone, and without any cement: its length is twenty-four feet, and its breadth fourteen. This was in former times the principal place of worship in the isle, and here they continue to bury their dead...

"In St. Kilda, at a distance of a mile from the village, and to the south-west, there is a chapel, in the language of the place called Brendan's temple: It has an alter within, and some Monkish cells without it. These are almost entire and must of consequence be of later date, than the holy places dedicated to Christ and Columba." (69-72).

According to oral tradition there once was a chapel on Boraraigh.

HARRIS

Teampall Bhrìghid NF 007928

This chapel was situated on the site of the present Scarista church, in the old graveyard, in the parish of Kilbride.

T.S. Muir (1885) says, "at Scarista… overlooking a long reach of sandy shore, is the modern church of Harris, and close by it the ancient burial-ground in which are a few old-looking gravestones, but no traces of the church which stood there, dedicated to St. Bridget." (44).

It is evident that this is an exceptionally old place of worship, but it does not seem likely that the old chapel will ever be found, although special individual stones can be seen in the old graveyard.

Teampall Mholuidh NB 2006

The Origines map (1851) identifies the site of a chapel as 'St. Malrube's' close to Màraig.

The Old Statistical Account (1794) mentions a chapel dedicated to 'St. Rufus'. No one is certain of the spot where the chapel was situated.

An Teampall, An Taobh Tuath

The name of Alasdair Crotach – one of the chiefs of MacLeod of Harris, who died in 1547 – is closely linked with the Harris chapels. And it is written that Alasdair Crotach built this chapel: that he built it at 'Nic Capevale', a few years before his death.

The walls and gables of the chapel are still intact, and it is situated in a beautiful spot by the shore, south of Ceapabhal.

The Royal Commission (1928) states, "It is a single chambered oblong structure, measuring 21 feet by 10 inches, with walls about 2⅔ feet thick." (31).

Above it and to the north can still be found the well called Tobar an t-Sagairt: there would surely have been priests associated with the chapel.

T.S. Muir (1885) says of this chapel, "Prettily situated on a green mound on the south side of the peninsula of Toe Head, and backed by Bein Chaipabhall, 1200 feet in height, stand the considerable remains of a chapel – in all likelihood one or other of the two spoken of in the 'Origines Parochiales' as having been dedicated to Saints Maelrubha and Luke." (44).

An Teampall, An Taobh Tuath

Tùr Mòr Chliamain

Tùr Mòr Chliamain NG 046832

This is the best-known chapel in the Western Isles, its architecture and design being distinct from the others.

In 1549 Dean Monro wrote, "In the south part of this isle lies a monastery with a steeple, which was founded and built by Macleod of Harris, called Rodel." (86).

This was Alasdair Crotach, who died two years previously and who is buried in a tomb inside the church – the tomb engraving being a renowned and powerful Highland icon.

The chapel was undoubtedly built on the site of a previous cell or church, but it was Alasdair Crotach who built it in its present form.

It was burnt to the ground when the Protestant faith arrived in the 16th century – as were many other churches – and nothing remained of the structure but the walls until they were rebuilt by the innovative Captain Alasdair MacLeod in the 18th century. One hundred years later it was again repaired.

A wealth of visual and oral information surrounds the totality of this chapel, and much of that defines the lives of the people of Harris through the centuries.

The islands are extremely fortunate that such an historic site exists, in order to give us a sense of historic place. (see Lawson, 1991; Macaulay, 1993; Royal Commission, 1928, 32-37).

An Teampall, An Scarp   NA 988137

This chapel was situated in the graveyard at Scarp, but little now remains of it.

The inhabitants of Scarp called the graveyard, 'An Teampall'.

It was Alasdair Crotach who also built this chapel, as well as St. Clement's and the chapel at Northton.

An 18th century account says, "Allister Crottach built two other beautiful Small Churches dependent on the monastery (St. Clement's) – one at Nic Capevale (Ceapabhal) and one in Scarp – now both in ruins." (see Duncan, 1995, 173).

Eaglais Tarain and Teampall Chè
                                      NG 031992

The sites of these two buildings are on Taransay.

Martin Martin talks of, "two chapels, one dedicated to St. Tarran, and the other to St. Keith." (123).

The Royal Commission (1928) says, "The stones having been removed, all that remains are two slight mounds within a few yards of the shore to the south-west of the township. Both chapels seem to have been oriented east and west, the mound of the western chapel, St. Keith's, measuring 21 feet in length by 12 feet in breadth, while that of the other, St. Taran's, which lies 38 yards to the east, is 32 feet long by 18 feet broad." (31).

Martin Martin gives an account of an unusual practice which the islanders followed in respect of the two graveyards, associated with both chapels: "There is an ancient tradition among the natives here that a man must not be buried in St. Tarran's, nor a woman in St. Keith's, because otherwise the corpse would be found above the ground the day after it is interred." (123).

Clach an Teampaill (NG 013008) is situated on the island, close to Uidh, but there is no sign of a chapel. (see Lawson, 1997).

Teampall na h-Annaid   NF 975847

The site of this chapel is in the old graveyard on the island of Killegray, above Caolas Sgàire. The Old Statistical Account (1791) states, "In the north end of the island of Calligray, there are faint traces of a very ancient building, called Teampall na h-Annaid… Near this temple is a well of water, at which the worshippers purified themselves, called Tobair na h-Annaid, and the point of land on which it is situated is called Ru na h-Annaid." (82).

The Royal Commission (1928) says, "It lies almost due east and west, and measures 21 feet in length by 12 feet in breadth internally, the mound of the wall being about 3 feet six inches thick. The door seems to have been in the centre of the western gable." (37).

One can also find Annaidean elsewhere: in Swainbost, and in Shader, Barvas; and in the Shiants.

Teampall Easaigh   NF 981866

This chapel was repaired and roofed in 1910 – around the same time as Teampall Mholuidh in Eoropie. Both were repaired by the Episcopalian Church, although that church had no previous links with them.

The Royal Commission (1928) states, "It is single chambered and oblong in plan, measuring 23 by 12 feet." (37).

All Martin Martin said was, "There is an old chapel here, for the use of the natives." (124).

Teampall Mhuire   NF 889869

This one is in the old graveyard at Baile na Cille in Pabbay.

Martin Martin relates, "There are two chappels on this island, one of which is dedicated to the Virgin Mary, the other to St. Moluag." (123).

They are referred to in the ONB as 'Teampall Mhoire' and 'Teampall Beag'. (Inverness, 5-7)

Part of Teampall Mhuire can still be seen, although the east gable has fallen. This was a large building, close to 40 feet long.

An unusual feature of this site is the way ground is shored up against these ruins, maybe because this site was a graveyard.

This is a peaceful, pleasant spot – on a beautiful and attractive island.

Teampall Mholuidh   NF 889870

This one is very close to Teampall Mhuire in Pabbay. It is much smaller, about 13 feet long. The east side is still intact. This one seems to be the older one.

Teampall Mholuidh   NF 913807

This chapel is located on the island of Berneray; in Cladh Mholuidh above the village of Borve.

Morrison (1989) states, "Its walls were standing in 1890 and its roof was formed apparently by stones gradually sloping to form a roof – like the old Irish celtic oratory. The walls were of course vandalised and little of it now appears above the ground." (60).

Cill Aiseam   NF 924826

This chapel is on the island of Berneray. The Old Statistical Account (1791) states, "There is a ruin in the island of Berneray, called, in the vitiated pronounciation of the people, Cill Aisaim…" (84).

The Royal Commission (1928) states, "No trace of the foundations of the church indicated by the name is now visible." (38).

Martin Martin refers to this chapel as 'St. Asaph's', and he mentions that there is an 8-foot-high standing stone close to it.

Morrison 1989 wrote, "St. Asaph… had a church dedicated to him in Berneray. Its sanctuary was marked by crosses in the middle ages... Near the site of the temple is a stone over 8 feet broad which has now fallen, but which was erect at the time Martin Martin visited the site..." (8).

NORTH UIST

Eilean an Teampaill NF 904707

This is a small island about two miles west of Lochmaddy: it is accessible at low tide. There is some kind of site there, but no certainty of there having been a chapel, and no knowledge of a name.

North of this, in Lochportain, there are three names – 'Loch an t-Sagairt', 'Cnoc Mòr an t-Sagairt' and 'Cnoc Beag an t-Sagairt' – but there is no sign of a chapel.

Teampall Chaluim Chille NF 873765

This site is in Clachan Shannda and by all accounts is very old.

Origines (1851) says, "Undoubtedly one of the two parish churches of North Uist mentioned by Dean Monro in 1549" (376). It is shown on Timothy Pont's map of 1600 as 'Kilchalmkil'. (Blaeu, 1654).

T.S. Muir (1861) wrote, "The west end of the chapel is standing, the rest of it greatly reduced, and partly buried under a huge sand-heap.' (225). Nowadays only the lower structure of the wall is visible in the east side of the graveyard: the graveyard is still in use. An extremely ancient site.

Half a mile to the south-east of the chapel there is a large stone (Martin Martin: "…about 8 feet high at Downrossel which the natives call a cross.") which has a number of names: 'Clach an t-Sagairt', Clach na h-Ulaidh', and 'Crois Adhamhnain' (St. Adamnan).

Tobar Chaluim Chille is situated a mile south of the chapel.

About 100 yards north of the chapel site there is a place called 'Druim na Croise'. MacRury (1950) states, "North of St. Columba Chapel on the Hornish end of 'Druim na Croise' there was a more ancient chapel dedicated to a St. Goulba." (14). Beveridge (1911) also mentions it.

Cladh Bhoraraigh   NF 855804

Although no sign can be seen of a chapel site on Boreray, 'Cladh nam Manach' can be seen on the OS map. Martin Martin wrote, "The Burial place near the Houses, is called the Monks-Field, for all the Monks that dyed in the Islands that lye Northward from Egg, were buried in this little plot." (69).

An Teampall, Orasaigh   NF 847757

Although a site was found on Orasaigh some years ago, no one is entirely sure that is was a chapel site.

The site is called 'Pàirce an Teampaill'.

Sgeilear, Sollas   NF 806757

The old Sgeilear graveyard is situated here, but there is no sign of a chapel ruin nor is there a chapel name now associated with it. MacCulloch (1824) gives the following account, "… an ancient chapel situated in the north west angle of the island." The east gable was still standing at that time, and was situated on a sand bank. Beveridge (1911) says, "The circumstantial account given by that writer (MacCulloch) cannot apply to any other locality than Skellor." (299).

Ard a' Mhorain   NF 837787

There is no evidence of the location of a chapel or any name associated with a chapel in the old graveyard at Ard a' Mhorain. But Tobar an t-Sagairt is situated above the shore about 200 yards west of the graveyard, and there is a cross carved out in the rock above it.

Teampall Mhuire   NF 786764

This is on Vallay Island, south of the old graveyard.

It is referred to by Martin Martin as, "It (Vallay) hath Three Chappels, One dedicated to St. Ulton, and another to the Virgin Mary." (67).

The Royal Commission (1928) states, "Only portions of the foundations remain… These foundations are confined to what seems to have been a chancel, about 9 or 10 feet square. The walling is 3 feet thick. A depression in the ground probably indicates the lines of a nave some three feet wider than the chancel." (51).

There were also two crosses in the vicinity. Beveridge found one of them in 1904, used as a lintel on the entrance to a burial aisle there. In 1885 T.S. Muir saw the other cross standing in the graveyard. Martin Martin had mentioned them both.

According to oral tradition there was once a nunnery on this island.

Teampall Ultain   NF 786763

Martin Martin mentions this chapel located on Vallay Island, although there is now no sign of it. It is thought to have been close to Teampall Mhoire. It is not mentioned in oral tradition or on the early maps. Chapels dedicated to St. Ultan are not at all common in Scotland.

Teampall Orain   NF 773771

This chapel is in Orasaigh, at the north-west point of Vallay Island.

The Royal Commission (1928) states, "On the west side of the peninsula of Oronsay are the foundations of a rectangular building lying east and west. The walls are dry built and about 4 feet thick, while the whole structure measures 24 by 17 feet internally." (50).

Beveridge (1911) states, "Adjoining the south side of this Teampall is some appearance of a semi-circular enclosure." (297).

Cille Pheadair   NF 726744

There is no sign now of this chapel, but it is known that it was located on the south side of a small hillock across from Balelone. It could be the one located on the John Speed map (1610) and referred to there as 'St. Patricius'.

Beveridge actually places it, "We are assured upon excellent authority that its burial ground has been recently exposed in course of ploughing the field. Its former site is indicated as a grassy plateau immediately to the south of Kilphedar Cross which now stands at the summit of the knoll, raised upon a modern square pedestal 6½ feet high. This cross was originally within the graveyard, having been removed to its present position by Dr. Alexander MacLeod (An Sgoilear Bàn) of Balelone about 1930-1840." (296).

Teampall Chliamain   NF 711728

This chapel site is situated in the old graveyard north of Tigharry.

On Blaeu's map (1654) and in Origines (1851) it is called 'Kilchalma' and 'Kilchalman', as if it were dedicated to St. Columba.

The ONB states, "It was dedicated to St. Clement and was a christening chapel & place of worship immediately preceding Kilmuir (the present parish church). (Inverness, 5-7).

The Royal Commission (1928) says, "The foundations of St. Clement's Chapel are still discernable. The building has been oblong, lying almost east and west, and measuring about 14 feet 6 inches in length and about 10 feet 9 inches in breadth internally. The door has been in the western gable." (50).

Cill Mhuire

NF 708706

This chapel was located in the graveyard south of Hogarry.

In Monro's time (1549) both this one and Teampall Chaluim Chille were the two parish churches in North Uist.

Oral tradition had it that the builders of this chapel were visited beforehand by a voice which instructed them: "Avoid Hough and Hosta, and build Cill Mhuire in Colasaidh." (The surrounding area is still called Colasaidh)

There is no evidence nowadays of this chapel but it is known that it was in the graveyard.

On Aird an Rùnaire, west of Cill Mhuire, there are two interesting names. 'Cladh Chòthain' is referred to as having been located on the east side of Aird an Rùnaire, but no site has as yet been found. There are a number of chapels dedicated to Còthan in the Highlands. And 'Eilean Trostain' is at the north side of Aird an Rùnaire: Trostan was closely linked to St. Columba.

Teampall Chrìosd

NF 783613

This chapel was in the graveyard at Baleshare and part of the west wall is still visible.

The Royal Commission (1928) states, "The foundations of the church, oblong on plan, are traceable with difficulty, but the building seems to have been about 42 feet long and about 12 feet broad internally, possibly with a divisional wall about 18 feet from the west end. It is orientated east by north and west by south…

"About 130 yards to the north-north-west is a conspicuous grassy ridge, known as Crois Mhor, while to the east is Creag Thormaidh, both supposed to be sanctuary limits." (49).

The local people are of the opinion that this is one of the churches built by Amie NicRuaraidh in Uist in the 14th century.

Tradition has it that there is a place called 'Baile na Cille,' in Iolaraigh, close to Teampall Chrìosd. (see Beveridge, 1911, 290).

Teampall na Trianaid   NF 816603

This is one of the large well-known island chapels, and a lot has been written about it.

Apparently a small chapel occupied the site in early times, although it did not enjoy the status of a parish church as did Teampall Mhuire in Cille Mhuire, and Teampall Chaluim Chille in Sannda. Teampall na Trianaid was re-built at least twice, and hardly anything remains of the original building.

According to tradition the chapel was built (or re-built) by Beathag, daughter of Somhairle, early in the 13th century, and it was repaired again by Amie NicRuairidh 150 years after that.

Although it has deteriorated, a substantial part of the walls still remains, which ensures that people are more aware of it than they are of any other old chapels in North Uist.

Teampall na Trianaid

The chapel housed large sculptured stones at one time, similar to those in Tùr Chliamain in Harris, but they are not there now.

This chapel has a lot of history attached to it: it was a university for priests, taught by a well-known family of professors – the MacVicars; it was burnt to the ground by Uisdean MacGilleasbaig Clèireach – one of the MacDonalds of Sleat – after the Reformation in the 16th century.

It is said that the acclaimed philosopher, Duns Scotus, was a student at this chapel. Tradition has it that it was used as a university up to the 17th century. (see Royal Commission, 1928; Beveridge, 1911; MacDonald, 1972).

Teampall Clann Mhic a' Phiocair

NF 816603

This building is attached to Teampall na Trianaid.

The Royal Commission (1928) states, "… a second structure, apparently a house and not a chapel, though known as Teampall MacVicar… The house is evidently subsequent (to the Teampall) and possibly dates from later in the 16th century." (48).

Heisgeir nan Cailleach

NF 645623

At the east side there is an old graveyard known as 'Cladh na Bleide' and about which Beveridge (1911) wrote, "It has almost certainly associated with a former chapel, of which no tradition seems now to remain although a slight wall is visible at the west base of a sand-hill." (291).

Tradition tells of a large monastery and of a large nunnery on Heisgeir.

MacRury (1950) says, "Heisker… is a place which had a long connection with Iona; it could boast a nunnery which continued to function till the time of the Reformation. A lighthouse now casts its warning beam over Eilean nam Manach, where, in days that are no more, nuns paid their devotions in the dim light of a seal-oil lamp… Up to about sixty years ago the site of the nunnery could be traced in the Ceann-an-Iar." (13).

Teampall Mhìcheil   NF 882548

This chapel is on the island of Grimsay in a place called Na Ceallan. It is situated on Rubha Mhìcheil with Eileanan an Teampaill some distance away.

It is confirmed that Amie NicRuairaidh built the chapel in the 14th century – as she built Teampall Chriosd in Baile Sear, and had repaired Teampall na Trianaid.

F.W. Thomas (1871) says, "the east wall being quite gone, and the south side, in which was the door, is but 3 feet high. There is 9 feet of the west wall left." (244).

Beveridge visited in 1905: "The north wall showed recent damage and was nowhere more than 3 feet high, without any appearance of the two windows mentioned by Captain Thomas." (1911, 279).

The Royal Commission (1928) states, "It is an oblong structure of stone and lime, orientated, and measuring internally 23 feet 2 inches in length by 13 feet 8 inches in breadth. The walls… are reduced to a height of about 1½ feet, except the western gable, which stands 8 feet high, and a small part of the south wall, which is 3 feet in height on the inside." (47).

Alexander Carmichael informs us that he found the site of another chapel in a small graveyard about 150 yards north of Teampall Mhìcheil.

Teampall Rònaigh NF 885572

The island of Rona lies to the east of the island of Grimsay. On the north-west side of the island one finds names such as Rubha an t-Sagairt and Beinn an t-Sagairt. There is also a spot called Cnoc nan Gall.

This ties in with what Martin Martin says, "a little Chappel in the Island of Rona, called the Lowlanders Chappel, because seamen who dye in time of Fishing, are buried in that place." (279).

BENBECULA

Teampall Chaluim Chille   NF 782549

This chapel is in Balivanich; it is on raised ground, surrounded by bog where Loch Chaluim Chille once was. At one time it was accessible by a path and it was surrounded by four crosses. Tobar Chaluim Chille is about 200 yards south-west of the chapel.

A large proportion of the walls is still intact, but little information on it is available.

It is marked on Timothy Pont's map of approximately 1600 as 'Kilcholambkil'.

The Royal Commission (1928) states, "The church has been oblong on plan, and, by a later extension, two-chambered, but the extent of the nave cannot definitely be ascertained, the side walls being breached… The total internal dimensions are 47½ feet from east to west by 14½ feet; the gables are 3½ feet thick, the eastern is reduced to the foundations, while the western remains to the height of the entrance lintel. The lateral walls, breached in places, stand on an average 8 feet above the present ground level." (99).

Origines (1851) says the following, "At Baillvanich (monk's town) on the north-west coast on a small island in a lake are remains said to be those of a monastery, but probably the remains of a chapel belonging to the monks of Iona." (370).

And T.S. Muir (1861) says, "A few yards off it, in a westerly direction, are the foundations of another oblong building, which was probably another chapel." (226).

Tradition tells us of how Teampall Chaluim Chille was built. St. Taran came ashore in the little bay in Balivanich which is called Callegeo. He wanted to build a chapel there, on Cnoc Feannaig, but the angels made him change the location to where it now is. The saint was also thirsty – he prayed and the lovely well, known as An Gàmhnach, over to the side of Ruaidhebhal, opened up. (see Carmichael, 1900, 80-83).

Teampall Mhuire   NF 765537

This chapel is in Nunton, in the old graveyard, Cille Mhuire. There is not much historical information available, apart from what visiting writers have written.

Martin Martin relates, "There is also some small Chappels here, one of them at Bael-nin-Killach." (150).

The Royal Commission (1928) says, "Within a graveyard at Nunton is the roofless shell of a small church, oblong on plan, built of rubble in mortar. It measures 24½ feet by 15½ feet over walls 2½ feet thick… The ruin is in fair condition, but the ground has silted up considerably." (99).

There is no sign at all of the building once occupied by nuns after which the place is named. According to the New Statistical Account, "In the island of Benbecula there

Teampall Chaluim Chille

was a nunnery on the farm called Nuntown. The building was taken down and the stones used in the building of Clanranald's mansion and office-houses." (188).

T.S. Muir (1861) has given the following information, "Nuntown, pleasantly situated about a couple of miles southward of Baile-manaich was the site of a nunnery, the remains of which were removed within the last forty or fifty years to build a 'mansion' for the last highland proprietor. In the adjacent burying-ground of Kilmuir, however, are preserved nearly entire the shell of the church of St. Mary." (226-227).

Griminis   NF 802518

It was said that there was a meeting-house here but that its stones were used to build an Established Church close by.

There is no information available about the original building.

Teampall Bhuirgh   NF 769503

This building has virtually disappeared into the machair land.

The Royal Commission (1928) says, "The ruined Teampull Bhuirgh, almost covered with blown sand, which reaches the top of the walls on the outside and partly fills the interior... It has been about 46 feet in length, and about 17 feet 10 inches in breadth internally. The gables have disappeared... and the inner face of the masonry has withered away." (100).

SOUTH UIST

Cill Amhlaigh NF 755463

The old graveyard of Kilaulay is near the village of that name west of Ardkenneth Church in Iochdar. The graveyard is marked on the Ordnance Survey map as, 'Burial Ground disused'. It was apparently in this graveyard that the meeting house called Cill Amhlaigh was situated. Donald John MacDonald (1981) wrote, "The small local churches were called meeting houses. This was before the Reformation." (12).

'Kileulay' is shown on Timothy Pont's map of Uist about 1600. (Blaeu, 1654).

West of 'Kileulay' on Pont's map, is 'Kilehainie': could there have been a meeting house there with a name like Cill Choinnich? And was it from there that the name Aird Choinnich came from?

Cille Bhanain

Loch Cille Bhanain lies west of Gerinish but there is no sign of the site of the actual cell. T.S. Muir (1861) mentions that there was once an old graveyard here although it is not now much in evidence. (227). It is named on the OS map as 'Chapel in ruins'.

Timothy Pont (1600) marks it on his map as 'Kiluanen'. (Blaeu, 1654). Martin Martin refers to it as 'St. Bannan'. (155).

The Royal Commission (1928) says, "It is oblong on plan, and is built almost due north and south. It measures some 54 feet in length, and 23 feet in breadth externally… It is in danger of collapsing in different places… The structure has been built partly on the site of a dun." (120).

Hoghmòr

This is one of the best known and most interesting sites in the whole of the Western Isles – it comprises not just one site, but a number. According to Monro (1549) both this one and Teampall Chille Pheadair were the two parish churches in South Uist.

Martin Martin says, "The churches here are St. Columba and St. Mary's in Hogh-more, the most centrical place in the island." (155).

T.S. Muir gives a detailed account of 5 separate buildings which comprise Hoghmòr although he does not name them all. The largest one is 60 feet long and he writes of it: "This was probably the ecclesia matrix of South Uist, and that

Hoghmòr

which is mentioned by Martin as under the dedication of St. Mary." (228).

When T.S. Muir returned after forty years he found the situation as follows: "Howmore at my first visit had remains of five churches and chapels, all standing close by one another. One of the number I now found had been removed during the late operation of inclosing the burial-ground… The missing one was a very characteristic building, the smallest of the group, with a very narrow rectangular window and a short sloping doorway in the east end. Externally it measured only 17½ feet in length." (280). This one was to the south of the large one furthest west; this was 'Caibeal nan Sagairt'.

Caibeal Chlann 'ic Ailein was at the north-west end of the graveyard.

The OS names three of the chapels: An Teampall Mòr; Caibeal nan Sagairt; and Caibeal Dhiarmaid.

Donald John MacDonald (1981) writes about Hoghmòr: "There were two churches in the parish of Howmore, St. Mary's church and St. Columba's. The remains of these two churches can be seen to the present day, and even the end wall of one of them is still standing…the old graveyard at Hoghmòr was the burial place of the Clanranalds, the area known as Caibeal Chlann 'ic Ailein." (12).

It was from here that the Clanranald stone was taken some years ago; it is now in the museum at Kildonan School.

MacDonald also added: "Added to the two large churches in Howmore, there was apparently an education college there, similar to Càirinis in North Uist, and the college and the churches, as well as St. Peter's church came under the authority of Iona." (12).

Cill Aird Mhìcheil
NF 7333

Nothing remains of this site, but it was apparently situated in the old graveyard out at Aird Mhìcheil.

Martin Martin refers to it as 'St. Mhìcheil'. (155).

Clachan a' Chumhaing
NF 7432

There is nothing left of this meeting house except the name.

Origines (1851) maps it as 'Clachan Cuay'. Donald John MacDonald (1981) calls it 'Clach a' Chumhaing'.

Cill Donnain
NF 731282

The OS map names this as 'Cill Donnain burial ground (disused)' on a point at the north-west end of Kildonan. It seems that the cell was located here although there is no evidence to that effect now.

'Kildonan' is mentioned in a paper in 1498 describing how King James IV was giving away land in South Uist. (Origines, 1851, 366).

The cell is named on Timothy Pont's map (1600) as 'Kildonan'. (Blaeu, 1654). Martin Martin refers to it as 'St. Donann'.

The Royal Commission (1928) states, "On a northerly projecting promontary on the west side of the northern half of Loch Kildonan is the site of Cill Donnain, but no trace of any building is now visible." (120).

Circeadal

All that is left of this chapel is the name, meaning the Dale of the Church. Origines (1851) calls it 'Kirkdale', and Donald John MacDonald (1981) mentions that one of the small meeting houses is "in Circedal to the south side of Loch Aoineirt." (13).

Cille Pheadair NF 735205

Kilpheder was the parish church for the south end of South Uist, as Howmore was the parish church in the north end. Dean Monro (1549) says, "The rest of the Ile callit Peiteris parochin, the parochin of Howf, and the mane land of the mid cuntrey callit Machermeanache." (76).

Although there is not much in evidence of it nowadays, it would seem that this was at one time a large and important chapel. It is referred to as early as the beginning of the 14th century, "In 1309 King Robert the Bruce granted… land in the parish of Kilpedire Blisen." (Origines, 1851, 366).

On Timothy Pont's map of Uist circa 1600, the church of 'Kilphedre' is depicted as being even larger than Hoghmòr. (Blaeu, 1654).

'Cladh Pheadair' is placed on the OS map half way between Loch na Liana Mòire and the shore. And the Royal Commission states, "About ¼ mile north of Loch a' Ghearraidh Dhubh, south-west of Daliburgh on the summit of a sand-hill, is Cladh Pheadair. No trace of the burial ground is now visible." (120).

An Teampall, Baghasdal

NF 7317

There is no certainty at present about the location of this chapel.

The ONB states, "A burial ground 1 mile south of North Boisdale and 1 mile north east of South Boisdale and is the supposed site of a chapel." (Inverness, 1878, 92).

Cill Choinnich

NF 796200

This one is on the OS map as 'Chapel & Cladh Choinnich (site of)'. The ONB says, "It is traditionally known that there once stood a chapel and a burying ground… But there is none now living who can point out with certainty the exact spot." (Inverness, 1878, 72).

The hill which is nowadays known as Beinn Ruigh Choinnich, east of the village of Lochboisdale, is referred to as 'Bin Kilohainie' by Timothy Pont (1600) – although the chapel itself is not on the Pont map. Neither Martin Martin nor Origines (1851) makes reference to it.

Cill Bhrìghde

NF 757141

This site was located in the village of Kilbride, at the south end of the island. It is on Timothy Pont's map (1600) as 'Kilvrid'. It is on the OS map as, 'Site of Cill Bhride (Burial ground)'.

MacDonald (1981) mentions that there was a little church at Kilbride.

The Royal Commission (1928) says, "In the old burying ground at Kilbride is the site of the ancient church of the same name, but all traces of it have been swept away." (120).

There is no information currently available on the following:

1. Martin Martin makes reference to 'St. Jeremy's Chapel' in South Uist.

2. Origines (1851) says, "The oldest men, says a writer of the seventeeth century, report this ile to be much empayred and destroyed be the sands ovirblowing and burieing habitable lands, and the sea hath followed and made the loss irreperable. There are destroyed the tounes and paroch churches of Kilmarchirmor and Kilpetil, that is, the church of the muir, for so it lay of old nearest the muirs, but now the sea and the sands have approached it. There be sum remaynes of the destroyed churches yit to be seen at low tydes or ebbing water." (368).

3. Origines (1851) maps a church to the east of Kildonan called 'Clachan of Branagh'. We have no information as to whether this linked up with Cladh Ard an Dugain which is marked on the OS map on a headland to the west of Loch Grianabreic in Airigh-Mhuilinn.

BARRA

Cille Bharra   NF 705074

This is a particularly important church.

Dean Monro (1549) refers to Barra as being, "with ane paroche kirke named Kilbarr." Timothy Pont (1600) maps it as 'Kilbarra'.

Martin Martin (1695) states, "The church in this island is called Kilbar, i.e., St. Barr's Church. There is a little chapel by it… The natives have St. Barr's wooden image standing on the alter, covered with linen in form of a shirt… (158).

"All the inhabitants observe the anniversary of St. Barr, being the 27th of September; it is performed riding on horseback, and the solemnity is concluded by three turns round St. Barr's Church. (163).

"They have likewise a general calvalcade on St. Michael's Day, in Kilbar village, and do then also take a turn round their church. Every family, as soon as the solemnity is ended, is accustomed to bake St. Michael's cake… and all strangers, together with those of the family, must eat the bread that night." (164).

Cille Bharra

The Royal Commission (1928) says, "the remains of a church and two dedicated chapels, grouped with the Church to the west and the chapels lying eastward and to either side... The church, which was dedicated to St. Barr, measures 38 feet by 13¼ feet within walls averaging 2½ feet thick. The gables are reduced almost to the ground level, but the side walls stand to a height of 7 or 8 feet... The northern chapel measures 26 feet by 9¾ feet... The third chapel measures 14½ feet by 8¼ feet." (123-124).

The 'northern chapel' – or Caibeal Mhuire – was re-roofed a few years ago, and ancient sculptured stones are retained there. It was here that the only runic stone ever to be seen in the Western Isles was found; it is now in the National Museum in Edinburgh.

To the east of Cille Bharra graveyard can be found the famous well called Tobar Bharra – an exquisite well with its sandy bottom. (see J.L. Campbell, 1936; Macquarrie, 1989).

Cill Bhrianain   NF 647017

The lower remains of this chapel are in the village of Borve along the shoreline.

The Royal Commission (1928) says, "In a burying ground on the south side of the low-lying peninsula terminating in Borve Point, just above the sea-shore, is a fragment of an old church, St. Brendan's Chapel, built of stone and lime... Only a small portion of a gable remains, standing about 3 feet in height, with part of the northern jamb of a door in position." (125).

Some of the written accounts refer to 'Cille Mhìcheil' as having been the name of this chapel. The Statistical Account (1794) says, "In Kilbar are two churches, built by the monks, belonging to Icolumkill; another at Borve, dedicated to St. Michael." (335).

T.S. Muir's account of the site (1885) is as follows, "It has been a building of very moderate size, consisting of a chancel and nave, respectively only 7 feet 10 inches and 23 feet in length, inside... I may mention, as perhaps worth recording, that the only other ecclesiastical building I have fallen in with in the Long Island in which the chancel and the nave are constructively separated, is the almost similarly proportioned church of St. John Baptist, at Bragar, on the west side of Lewis." (282).

THE BISHOP'S ISLES

To the south of Barra lie the Bishop's Isles;
Dean Monro (1549) identifies nine islands and
tells that each one of them had a chapel – Lingay;
Gigarun; Berneray; Megaly (Mingulay); Pabay;
Fladay; Scarpnamut (Muldonaich); Sanderay;
Watersay. Monro says, "All thir nine Iles forsaid
had a Chapell in every Ile." (72-73).

Cille Bhrianain   NL 664957

This chapel is on the east side of Vatersay, in Uineasain. It is
also called, "Caibeal Moire nan Ceann'. The story is told of
Moire having been a wild woman, beheading anyone who
was not to her liking. She was from the Isle of Coll, and she
wished to be buried in full view of that island. The funeral
procession became weary of carrying her and they buried her
in Uineasain although Maoldònaich is between her resting
place and Coll.

The Royal Commission (1928) comments, "… an old
burying ground containing the foundations of an old church
of stone and lime… The building has been oblong and
oriented east-north-east and west-south-west. It has been
about 37 feet long and 16 feet 6 inches broad externally."
(137).

Cille Bhrìghde

This chapel was situated on Sandray.

The Royal Commission (1928) says, "In an old burying ground above the shore to the south-east of Bagh Ban, near the north-east corner of Sandray, are faint traces of the ancient chapel of Cille Bhride. The larger part of the site is occupied by a sheep fank, but a corner of its foundations built of stone and lime can be detected." (137).

The chapel has now completely been engulfed by sand.

Cill, Pabaigh

The name of this island – and every other island with the same name – means a place where a monk resided at one time. And Monro says that there was a chapel on this island as was on all the others round about.

The Royal Commission (1928) says, "On what is now a mound some 10 feet high, on the south-western border of the sandy slope running up from Bagh Ban on the eastern shore of Pabbay, about 150 yards from the high-water mark, are the indistinct foundations of an oblong church of stone and lime measuring 31 feet in length and 14 feet in breadth externally, and oriented slightly north of west and south of east." (126).

It is not easy to find this site; the sand has engulfed it over the years.

The singular Pictish stone of the Western Isles was found here during the twentieth century, and other stone slabs with crosses on them were also found.

Cill Chaluim Chille

NL 565833

This chapel was located on Mingulay.

The Royal Commission of (1928) says, "No traces of St. Columba's Chapel are to be seen. It stood above the shore at the north-west corner of Mingulay Bay, a sandy bay on the east-side of the island." (137).

Buxton (1995) tells that, "The officers of the Ordnance Survey were informed in 1878 of the traditional site of a chapel, dedicated to St. Columba, with graveyard attached. This was the knoll, occupied by the graveyard, next to the stream in the village, and the corner of a building is now visible on the knoll… Graveyards on all four of the other main islands south of Barra (Bhatarsaigh, Sanndaigh, Pabaigh agus Beàrnaraigh) are similarly the traditional sites of chapels, though only on Mingulay are there visible remains." (31).

Cill, Beàrnaraigh

NL 567803

This chapel was located on the Isle of Berneray, but the name is not now known.

The Royal Commission (1928) says, "Near MacLean's Point some 350 yards east by south of the landing jetty on the island of Bernera and about 50 yards from the shore in an old burying ground is the site of a church, all traces of which have disappeared." (137).

If anything is left of the building, it has been engulfed by sand long ago.

A stone slab with an engraving of a cross was found near at hand: it was at least 1,000 years old.

At the end of his journey through the islands, T.S. Muir arrived at Bernera on the 15th of July 1866. Although he did not find any signs of the old graveyard and the chapel, he rested, "Bernera – Here, after innumerable jumblings by land and sea, I am – thanks for it! – at the end of my journey, and taking a few days' rest in the lighthouse." (1885, 254). What a fortunate man.

BIBLIOGRAPHY

John Barber, 1987, Innsegall: The Western Isles. John Donald.

Erskine Beveridge, 1911, North Uist.

Ben Buxton, 1995, Mingulay. Birlinn.

John Lorne Campbell et al, 1936, The Book of Barra. Routledge.

Alexander Carmichael, 1972, Carmina Gadelica.
    Scottish Academic Press.

Ian B. Cowan, 1967, The Parishes of Medieval Scotland.
    Scottish Record Society.

Frank Fraser Darling, 1939, A Naturalist on Rona. Oxford.

Angus Duncan, 1995, Hebridean Island. Memories of Scarp.
    Tuckwell Press.

James Hogg, 1888, A Tour in the Highlands in 1803. Gardner.

Bill Lawson, 1991, St. Columba's Church at Aignish; 1991,
    St. Clements Church at Rodel; 1993, St. Kilda and its Church;
    1994, The Temple on the Isle of Pabbay; 1997,
    The Isle of Taransay. Bill Lawson Publications.

John Macaulay, 1993, Silent Tower. Pentland.

Murdo MacAulay, c1984, Aspects of the Religious History of Lewis.

Kenneth MacAulay, 1764, The History of St. Kilda. James Thin.

John McCulloch, 1824, The Highlands & Western Isles of Scotland.
    Longman.

Dr. MacDonald of Gisla, 1967, Tales and Traditions of the Lews. Mrs MacDonald.

Donald Macdonald, 1978, Lewis; A History of the Island. Gordon Wright.

Dòmhnall Iain MacDhòmhnaill, 1981, Uibhist a Deas. Acair.

Norman Macdonald, 1972, Trinity Temple, North Uist.

W.C. MacKenzie, 1903, The History of the Outer Hebrides; 1932, The Western Isles. Gardner.

Finlay Macleod (ed), 1989, Togail Tir. Acair/An Lanntair.

Alan Macquarrie, 1989, Cille Bharra. Grant Books.

Ewen MacRury, 1950, A Hebridean Parish. Northern Chronicle Office.

Martin Martin, 1934 , A Voyage to St. Kilda; A Description of the Western Isles of Scotland. Eneas Mackay.

Dean Monro, 1549, Western Isles of Scotland. (ed. R.W. Munro, 1961, Oliver and Boyd).

Alick Morrison, 1989, The Island of Berneray and its History.

T.S. Muir, 1861, Characteristics of Old Church Architecture; 1885, Ecclesiological Notes on Some of the Islands of Scotland David Douglas.

Origines Parochiales Scotiae, 1851. Lizars.

Ordnance Survey Original Object Name Books (ONB).

D.D.C. Pochin Mould, 1953, West Over Sea. Oliver & Boyd.

Michael Robson, 1991, Rona; The Distant Island. Acair.

Royal Commission, 1928, Ancient and Historical Monuments of Scotland: The Outer Hebrides, Skye and the Small Isles. HMSO.

NOTES

NOTES

NOTES

The
Healing Wells

photographs
Donald John Campbell

INTRODUCTION

People have always been mindful of water for it is at the heart of all living matter. It is therefore no surprise that it has been viewed as a resource with powerful properties, and as something to which mankind has strong attachment. Consequently importance was attached to locations which held water – such as lochs, rivers and wells or springs. These locations nearly always emanate a sense of beauty, but people have been aware that they are also special places, and in a sense people viewed them as living locations – alive with their own particular spirit, as were many other phenomena in their world.

People have therefore come to associate wells with strength and succour, believing that they would receive assistance, information and advice from them. But in order to receive this, they had to approach the wells in a particular way, and they had to adhere closely to associated customs. If they did not do so, the live spirit of the well would not be able to assist them.

Banks (1937) wrote: "Wells, springs, streams and pools have been accredited with healing powers, wherever man has had ailments to cure, and Scotland with its numerous mountains and glens was famed more than many other lands for healing waters. Long before the Christian era, springs endowed with magical virtue were regarded as bringers of health from the heart of the earth." (125).

It is rather difficult for us nowadays to imagine ourselves in these situations, and to understand how people perceived their world and its mode of operation. Nobody nowadays ascribes a living power to the physical environment as was the case in times past. As a result, neither wells nor such special places hold any potency for them, and these sites cease to be meaningful and are forgotten about.

But this was not always the case. Many hundreds of wells were located throughout the country and it is estimated that there were at least six hundred healing wells throughout Scotland – with people being very much aware of them and affording them high status. Many of these wells were named after different saints such as St Columba, St Andrew, St Ronan and many others. Linked with Christianity there were also many small chapels in differing locations and sometimes wells were associated with these chapels (See MacLeod, 1997). This illustrates how the people viewed the wells as spiritual sanctuaries which were closely linked to the chapels. The wells served as a visible part of how people imposed a pattern on the world in which they lived and of the spiritual sense which guided their understanding of that world.

As part of their beliefs the daily lives of the people were heavily influenced by oral tradition. They expressed their philosophy through that oral tradition and, as expected, water and well occupied their own place within that tradition, with many tales and traditions linked to some of these wells.

Different people have written accounts of the many customs connected with wells and the confidence that people had in them. Arthur Mitchell (1880) wrote: "The adoration of wells may be encountered in Scotland from John O' Groats to the Mull of Galloway. I have seen a dozen wells in Scotland that have not ceased to be worshipped. Nowadays, the visitors are comparatively few, and those who go are generally in earnest. The object is usually the restoration to health of some poor little child. Indeed the cure of sick children is a special virtue of many of these wells." And J.F. Campbell wrote in Popular Tales of the West Highlands (1892): "Holy healing wells are common all over the Highlands; and people still leave offerings of pins and nails and bits of rag, though few would confess it. There is still a well in Islay where I myself have, after drinking, deposited copper caps amongst a hoard of pins and buttons and similar gear placed in chinks in the rocks and trees at the edge of the 'Witches' Well'." (2, 145).

There were wells located throughout the Western Isles, often with specific names, and with information and customs associated with them. Although this knowledge has withered over the years, a good deal of it still remains, and it is this knowledge which this small book seeks to bring together. There is not the same interest now in wells as once existed; people's views on such topics have greatly altered. People nowadays do not have the same vision of the world as was once prevalent and because of this the detailed knowledge of places and wells which once existed is no more. Despite that, wells are still to be found in the Western Isles, with associated tales which give an example of the beliefs which were common about wells throughout the country.

For example, it was said that it was offensive to the spirit of the well if that spirit was insulted in any way. The well could move on account of it or close up. Oral tradition has it that Tobar Thòmais in Geàrrannan could move if a cow were to excrete too close to it, and the spirit of Tobar Thiobartan moved because a man took his one-eyed horse there for a cure. Martin Martin has a particular account of a well in Colonsay which fled to Islay: "A mile on the south-west side of the cave Uah Vearnag is the celebrated well called Toubir-in-Knahar, which, in the ancient language, is as much as to say the well has sailed from one place to another; for it is a received tradition of the vulgar inhabitants of this isle, and the opposite isle of Colonsay, that this well was first in Colonsay, until an impudent woman happened to wash her hands in it, and that immediately after, the well being thus abused, came in an instant to Islay, where it is like to continue, and is ever since esteemed a catholicon for diseases by the natives and adjacent islanders, and the great resort to it is commonly every quarter-day. It is common with sick people to make a vow to come to the well, and after drinking it they make a tour sunways round it, and then leave an offering of some small token, such as a pin, needle, farthing, or the like, on the stone cover which is above the well. But if the patient is now like to recover they send of the water to be drunk by the sick person. There is a little chapel beside the well, to which such as had found the benefit of the water, came back and returned thanks to God for their recovery." (274).

By the same token, a dog must not drink from one of the wells in Uamh Uladal, or it would dry up as a result. It was said that some wells had an ability to foretell the future: the most notable well with such properties in the Western Isles being Tobar Anndrais in Siadar, which could give an indication whether patients would survive their illness. Also some people verified their love vows at wells or requested that they should enjoy good luck – Tobar Chaluim Chille in Tangasdal was one such well.

Other singular accounts were given of wells – one which would not whiten linen, and one whose water could not be boiled. Some others carried the name of 'tobar nam buadh', or well of virtues, and there are two such wells in the Western Isles – one in Kismul Castle and a particularly notable one in St. Kilda. The Gaels referred to delicious water by using the word 'wine' and there is one well called 'tobar creag an fhìon' (well of the wine rock) in the Western Isles, in South Uist.

Some wells commanded great respect because of their curative powers for the treatment of mental illness. On mainland Scotland, two wells in particular are associated with such curative powers. There are Tobar Mhaolruibhe on the island of Maolruibhe and the spa at St Fillans. In an early account of Tobar Mhaolruibhe Pennant (1774) states: "The curiosity of the place is the well of the saint; of power unspeakable in cases of lunacy." (330). Each person suffering from mental illness who sought a cure at the well drank from it and stuck coins in a tree beside the well, and the patient had then to be dragged round the island tied to a boat. Arthur Mitchell, who visited the well in 1880, wrote:

"One of the things which the Presbytery of Dingwall (in the mid-17th Century) deplored and sought to suppress was the adoration of wells. Now, in certain aspects, this adoration of wells continues largely to our day. Even the very well on Innis Maree, which the Dingwall Presbytery had prominently in view at their meeting on the 5th of September 1656, still receives adoration. When I visited it some fifteen years ago, I found numerous offerings fastened to the tree which stands beside it." (149).

The well has now dried up but people still stick coins in the surrounding trees. It was only once a year that patients suffering from mental illness were taken to the St Fillans waters to seek a cure.

The water in Tobar Chùisdein in Point falls into the sea, and oral tradition (and Martin Martin) relates that patients with mental illness found relief if they stood for a while under the stream falling from the well. People travelled long distances to seek relief. But the best account available of this phenomenon is in connection with Tobar an Teampaill/ Tobar Rònain and Teampall Mholuaidh in Eòrapaidh. Oral Tradition in Ness has been strong in giving an account of activities surrounding the chapel and the well. Martin Martin collected information about these customs. The patient was brought to this place and he had to drink and be baptised with the water from the well, and he had to go sunwise round the chapel and spend the night bound beside the altar, and his chances of recovery were higher if he were able to sleep. Many other stories about this site are still in existence: in ancient times in Ness this location was a prime revelation of the mysterious world which the people inhabited.

Well water was also thought to be a cure for epilepsy. But there was an added element connected with this and that was a human skull. A visit was made to the graveyard during the hours of darkness where a skull was dug up and brought home. Water was then taken from a healing well and the patient drank the water from the skull. The skull had to be returned that same night. People were generally of the opinion that the skull of someone who had taken their own life was the most effective. A tale similar to this was told in Borgh, Lewis. Anne Ross (1966) wrote: "The skull of a suicide, often filled with water from a holy well, was a known and much-believed-in cure for epilepsy, but it was held in reserve for a final measure, when all other, less dramatic, remedies had failed. In Lewis, the skull of an ancestor would be dug up from a special place in the graveyard, after sunset and before sunrise, and water placed in it from a sacred well; this was then taken to the patient and he or she had to drink it, the whole ritual, from beginning to end, being performed in silence." (80-81).

The Rev. William Matheson gave the following account to Anne Ross (1962) in connection with skulls and wells: "A similar tradition was still current in comparatively recent years in the island of Lewis. An elder of the United Free Church in Ness had an epileptic daughter. He eventually decided to try to cure her of epilepsy in a traditional manner. Between sunset and sunrise and without speaking to a living thing, he walked five miles to the family burial-ground at Teampull Chrò Naoimh at North (sic) Galson. There he dug up the grave and removed the skull from it. He came back home with the skull, awakened the epileptic girl and made her drink from the skull. He then walked back to Teampull Chrò Naoimh to re-bury the skull. My informant did not know the name of the well from which the water was taken, but it is likely to have been a healing well and its name should still be ascertainable." (36-37). There is no definite evidence as to the location of the well referred to.

The Gaels believed that the human head had particular powers. In a manner of speaking they worshipped the head, and it often appeared in their art. It is not surprising therefore that they were of the opinion that a head would strengthen the healing properties of a well, and as a consequence human heads were placed in wells. This custom dates very far back in the history of the Celts as a people. Anne Ross (1976) writes: "It was a powerful and ancient Celtic belief, of which there are many examples, that by placing a human head in a venerated well, the powers of the water – whatever they were, healing in general, effecting specific cures, imparting fertility, and so on – were markedly increased by the magic powers with which the human head was accredited in the Celtic world down the centuries." (81).

The one example that we know of in the Western Isles of 'tobar nan ceann' or well of the heads, is to be found in Barra, and Nan MacKinnon often spoke of it. It is noteworthy that this ancient Celtic belief is still to be found in the Western Isles down to the present day. Examples of 'tobar nan ceann' are to be found throughout Scotland.

It was also from Barra that the remarkable tale of cockles being found in a fresh water well originated and much has been written on the topic. There is no trace of this having arisen anywhere else other than in Barra except that Boece (1527) located his version in Mull: it seems as if this tale was passed from one writer to another.

There are one or two examples in the Western Isles of rain water being collected in hollows in stones – these are 'Tobar nan Cupan' and 'Tobar na Reulaig'. Cup-stones and receptacles in stone slabs are known to have been used to collect rain water for use as a cure for disease of the eyes and illnesses such as whooping-cough. Little is known of these remedies in the Western Isles today.

Most of the healing qualities of wells were associated with illness or toothache. There were many toothache wells throughout the Western Isles at one time, and a number are still known. Whether it was the coldness of the water which dulled the toothache or whether the walk to the well acted in a therapeutic way is not known. Whatever it was, the people believed that the water from these wells was effective in curing the pain of toothache. Very definite customs have been passed down showing them how to approach each particular well; very often it had to be early in the morning, before they had eaten, and they must not utter a word to another living person on their way to the well or on the way back. Some wells had their own associated customs as to how many mouthfuls should be consumed: for example, Tobar an Dèididh in Cnoc Ard in Ness, where seven mouthfuls had to be taken, with the first six being spurted back out on a stone but with the seventh one being swallowed.

Many wells were also visited to effect a cure for all sorts of aches, pains and illnesses, from a sore stomach to eye complaints and diabetes. There was also the belief of elderly people who were experiencing the loss of their energy and vigour: in their hospital bed and often on their death bed they craved for a cold mouthful of water from a healing well with which they had been acquainted in their childhood. Physicians often encouraged them to do this. Again we do not know whether these were cases of faith healing or whether minerals such as iron or sulphur in the water strengthened them while in their weak state. Many had a craving for a 'drink of the cold water' – water which was 'cold on a hot summer's day and warm on a cold winter's day', emanating from the depths of the earth.

Usually people had learnt that they ought to leave a token at the well if they were going to ask a favour. The act was everything – the value of the token was irrelevant.

There are at least two explanations as to why tokens were left beside the wells. It could have been a gift for the spirit of the well, giving thanks for the cure which the spirit had bestowed through the medium of water, or that one had to make a gesture of payment before the spirit of the well would heal. But many believed that the patient was leaving a bit of himself there, as a symbol of the pain or ill health that he was leaving behind him. Probably both reasons were linked together, at least sometimes.

People felt they could leave any kind of items beside the well as an offering. It might seem to us that the little insignificant articles which were left have no meaning or sense; at times these were little stones or tufts of heather which they gathered on their way to the well.

Nowadays we tend to see bits of clothing hanging on trees close to some wells. That, or coins, where there are wishing wells. In the centre of the quadrangle of the university with which I myself am most acquainted, you can see many coins at the bottom of the well at examination time!

Through the wells we are able to see vestiges of customs which were at one time widespread throughout the land. Water was seen as a live and powerful element, and people were drawn to it although they were also in awe of it. The knowledge they had was knowledge of how they could attain health and wholesomeness through the power associated with water and wells. Although the nature of people's information has changed since those times, there are still remnants of ancient knowledge in existence, and some of the wells are still known, bearing witness to thought processes that are today not easy to penetrate.

THE WELL

Derick Thomson

Right in the village there's a little well
and the grass hides it,
green grass in sap closely thatching it.
I heard of it from an old woman
but she said: "The path is overgrown with bracken
where I often walked with my cogie,
and the cogie itself is warped."
When I looked in her lined face
I saw the bracken growing round the well of her eyes,
and hiding it from seeking and from desires,
and closing it, closing it.

"Nobody goes to that well now,"
said the old woman, "as we once went,
when we were young,
though its water is lovely and white."
And when I looked in her eyes through the bracken
I saw the sparkle of that water
that makes whole every hurt
till the hurt of the heart.

"And will you go there for me,"
said the old woman, "even with a thimble,
and bring me a drop of that hard water
that will bring colour to my cheeks."
I found the well at last,
and though her need was not the greatest
it was to her I brought the treasure.

It may be that the well
is something I saw in a dream,
for today when I went to seek it
I found only bracken and rushes,
and the old woman's eyes are closed
and a film has come over their merriment.

An Dealbh Briste, 1951.
(Creachadh na Clàrsaich, 1982)
(Translated by the author from the Gaelic original)

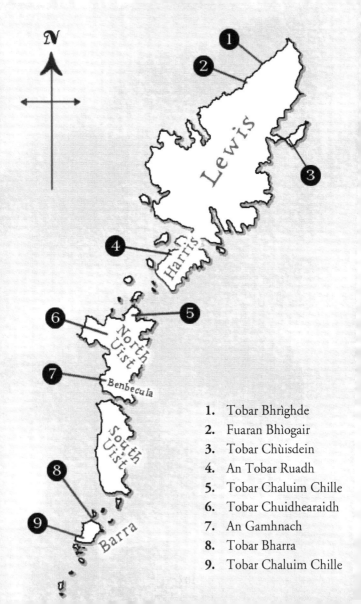

1. Tobar Bhrìghde
2. Fuaran Bhìogair
3. Tobar Chùisdein
4. An Tobar Ruadh
5. Tobar Chaluim Chille
6. Tobar Chuidhearaidh
7. An Gamhnach
8. Tobar Bharra
9. Tobar Chaluim Chille

LEWIS

Fuaran Stoth NB 523659

This spring is to be found in Ness to the west of the road above Stoth bay, close to the Butt of Lewis. This well has iron properties and the local custom was for people to visit it in order to get a cure for stomach problems, as well as to generally get a feeling of wellbeing, having partaken of the water. It is not all that long since people gave up visiting this well.

Fuaran an Dèididh NB 535650

This spring is situated at Geodh nan Cruidh by the shore at Cnoc Ard, across from the north face of Dun Eistean. This was one of the toothache wells and people visited it to get relief from toothache. A person suffering from toothache would take seven mouthfuls from it and would spurt out six of these on a stone situated beside the well, but would drink the seventh mouthful.

MacPhail gives a different account: "At Duneistein, near the Butt of Lewis, there is a well at the base of a high rock quite close to the sea, which goes by the name of 'Fuaran an dèididh', Toothache Well, and which is supposed to cure the toothache. The cure consists in taking in succession three mouthfuls of the water in this well, which are to be kept in one's mouth as long as convenient. Then each mouthful is to be spurted out on a large stone in a cave close to hand, on which the sun never shines. People afflicted with toothache still resort to Fuaran an dèididh for cure. The writer, in the sixties (1860s), was persuaded to do so." (MacPhail was from Shawbost: he was in Ness as a Gaelic teacher at that time.).

In the last few years the force of the sea has caused this well to close and has also caused the stone to disappear.

Tobar Rònain/Tobar an Teampaill NB 518649

This well is situated by the road in Eòrapaidh and the local people saw it as having a link with two chapels – St. Moluag's and St. Ronan's, both of which were close by.

At one time people suffering from mental illness were taken to St Moluag's. It was believed that people in this state would be cured if they slept for one night tied to the church altar. The person had to come to the church at nightfall and go round it sunwise seven times. The person then had to drink water from the well and had to also be baptised with water from it. The water was carried in a small receptacle, and that receptacle was in the custody of a family who were descendants of 'the clerks of the temple'.

This information had been handed down through tradition bearers and through the written word. Arthur Mitchell (1862), who was a lunacy inspector for the whole of Scotland wrote: "Lunatics are brought from many parts of the north-west of Scotland to this ruin. One man who had been taken there, and whom I saw, had the good fortune to sleep, and was cured. He afterwards married, and had a family. Seven years ago he again became insane, and I found him labouring under dementia. I heard of several others in our own day, who had been sent to St Molonah (sic) – some from the mainland of Scotland – but no happy issue was reported. A Lewis gentleman, reading this paper in manuscript, writes on the margin: "I know two persons who were brought to the temple. The result was favourable, but one has had a return of the malady. It is said that a visit to the church has no efficacy for a return of the disease." (268). MacPhail was in Ness as a young teacher and he gives a particular account of the practice: "One of my earliest recollections in connection with the temple was one day, hearing people remarking that a young man, whose mind happened to be unhinged at the time, had been seen passing through the district in which I lived, in the custody of his friends, on his way to 'Teampull-Eoropie'. I was slightly acquainted thirty-five years ago with the individual in question. He was then quite sane."

Fuaran nam Maoim NB 556568

This spring is on the Ness moor. Two brothers from Lionel erected a cement covering for it. Murdo Maclean from Habost, Ness wrote: "A little bit further out from Gil Sgioba-Gearraidh was Airigh nam Maoim, and there was a spring there from which people used to drink, thinking it was good for this and that. It was full of iron.

Fuaran a' Ghròdhair NB 510637

This spring is beside the Swainbost river, inside the farmhouse wall, close to sands and machair land. People used to take water from it to treat toothache.

Tobar Bhrighde

Tobar Chliamain   NB 490624

This well was in North Dell, close to the site of Teampall Chliamain, south of Arnaistean. Nobody nowadays has any information on it, and nothing was written about it.

Tobar Bhrìghde   NB 411574

This well is close to St Brigit's cemetery in Melbost, Borve. It is done up with cement, and people still use it. It has a narrow entrance but still wide enough to accommodate a small cup. The water in this well was effective in the treatment of jaundice.

Fuaran an Dèididh   NB 4056

According to Peter Smith from Borve, this spring was to be found in at the shore on the croft closest to the Borve river, and to the west side of it. It was visited first thing in the morning and nobody must see the person actually visiting it. He said it was a small well.

Tobar Anndrais   NB 384554

This is one of the most important wells in the Western Isles. It was Martin Martin who first described it: "St Andrew's well, in the village of Shader, is by the vulgar natives made a test to know if a sick person will die of the distemper he labours under. They send one with a wooden dish to bring some of the water to the patient, and if the dish, which is then laid softly upon the surface of the water, turn round sun-ways, they conclude that the patient will recover of that distemper; but if otherwise , that he will die." (90).

This once famous well is nowadays filled up with stones and a fence-post.

Fuaran an Dèididh   NB 381554

This spring is down on the shore line north west of Teampall Pheadair. A nearby slope has long since fallen and concealed the well, which is no longer to be seen.

Tobar Mhoire   NB 382550

This well is also known as Tobar Mhòr and/or Tobar Eire. It is at the roadside at Mol Eire. Although people are still aware of its existence they do not recall its association with healing qualities.

Fuaran Bhìogair   NB 347519

This spring is situated in a cleft in a rock at the shore at Bhìogair. It always contains bracing cold water. It was used to cure toothache and also to help relieve those suffering from mental illness.

Fuaran Bhiogair

Fuaran Bhinnisgro/Ghuinnisgro   NB 355483

This well is situated on the Barvas Moor at the west of the river, approximately a mile south west of the village. It is a large well – about a foot wide and about two feet in length, with yellow/brown sides. Beside it stands a lovely white stone.

According to Peter MacLeod of Barvas, those suffering from diabetes or stomach pains used to come to it. People used to regurgitate what they had drunk from it, and this gave them relief. Its water was also used to relieve rheumatism.

Fuaran an Talaimh Mholaich   NB 305485

This spring is among the crofts, at Cnoc an Ois to the west of Arnol village. It was recognised as having qualities to relieve those suffering from stomach pain. The late Dr Ross used to give water from this well to those complaining of stomach pains.

Every Sunday, the young men of the village used to visit this well carrying a flask in their pocket.

Fuaran Buaile Dhòmhnaill   NB 289486

This spring was situated in croft-land among the furrows of oats and barley, about 200 yards south of Teampall Eòin. It might have been the well used by those associated with that church in days gone by. It was in a hollow among the grass, and measured about three feet wide. A lively spring of water arose from its centre, and a film, resembling oil, was to be seen on the surface.

Water from this well was brought to those who were ill; sometimes to those who were patients in the Lewis Hospital. According to Aonghas Phàdraig from Bragar, its water was also used to cure toothache.

Round about 1980, it was completely destroyed by a JCB.

Fuaran Gharson   NB 264485

This spring is to be found in a stony bay at Garson in Shawbost: the spring is in a cleft at the foot of the cliff and on the left as you descend. Often if there is a storm it fills up with pebbles.

People used to visit this well to improve their health. The Ordnance Survey Word Book describes it as: "Apparently a kind of spa."

Tobar 'ic Thòmais/Tobar Bhalabhair
NB 198446

This well is known by two names. It is situated in the moorland, to the east of the village of Geàrranan. It contains lime. Stories are still told of people visiting this well to get water for those who were ill. Bottles of water were brought to those who were ill in hospital. Accounts are given of how the water was brought to those on their deathbed: they craved for it.

It was said that if a cow excreted close to the well it would spring up in another location.

Tobar Chiarain NB 185426

This well is down in Laimsiadar, to the east of a bend in the wall which runs across the neck of the headland. Martin Martin also describes it: "A well at Loch Carlvay, that never whitens linen, which hath often been tried by inhabitants." (90).

Teampall Chiarain was situated close by, and also Stighe Chiarain descending close to it.

It was said that people came and went on their knees at Càrn a' Bheannaich, which is close at hand, and that the priest used to bless them with water from Tobar Chiarain. They would then place their head on a stone and sleep after they had been thus blessed, and that this stone was a special stone.

MacPhail wrote in the Oban Times in 1898: "Anyone with a lingering disease was taken to Ciaran's shrine. Walked deiseil (sunwise) round the temple. Whatever the ailment, if he could be induced to sleep in the church he was sure to begin forthwith to improve." This is very similar to Martin Martin's account of Teampall Mholuaidh in Eòropaidh.

Tobar Chiarain NB 194428

Strangely this is a second well in Carloway named after Ciaran. This one is situated in croft land, and although it bears the name of a saint, no one has any recollection of whether people went there to seek a cure for illness.

Tobar Càrn an Dòbhrain   NB 342207

This well can be found at Aird a' Chaolais to the north west of Cliacabhagh in the north of Calanais. It is situated in the moorland and it seems as though it is a well with water strong in iron. People used to visit it because of its healing properties; as was often the case they compared its water to the waters of Strathpeffer (An Tobar).

Fuaran Tràigh Theinis   NB 117353

This spring is also called the toothache well. It is situated in a cleft measuring approximately one foot wide in the rock above the shore to the west of Stung close to Tràigh Theinis in Riof, Uig. Sometimes it is full of black seaweed, but once it is cleaned out, the water is beautifully clear. It is surrounded by lime.

Tradition has it that it had to be visited on an empty stomach first thing in the morning. The person had to be accompanied but no conversation had to take place either on the way there or back. Three mouthfuls had to be taken; the first two had to be spurted into the sea and the third one was swallowed.

Tobar a' Bheannachaidh   NB 038378

This sacred well was close to Taigh a' Bheannaich, to the west of Aird, Uig. T.S. Muir (1885) makes reference to it, but there is no mention of it in oral tradition nowadays.

Fuaran an Dèididh
NB 037334

This well can be found in Crabhlasta, at Creag Reithamul, near Port Bhasdair. It is in the cleft of a rock above the shore. It was visited to bring relief to those suffering from toothache.

Fuaran Bhaile na Cille
NB 047338

In the cemetery there once was a church called Teampall Chrìosd; Martin Martin referred to it as 'St Christopher's chapel in Uge'. And TS Muir (1885) says of the spring: "At Uig, 8 miles north of Mealastadh, there is a well called Tobar Nec Cieres, but no remains of the ancient church which was dedicated to Saint Christopher." (40-41).

Fuaran Gheòdabrigh
NB 542462

This spring can be found on the shore south of the pier in North Tolsta. Its water was used as a cure for sore eyes. Sufferers wiped their eyes with the water.

Tobar Chùisdein
NB 514337

It was Martin Martin's account which highlighted this well in Point: "St Cowsten Church. The well there never boils meat of any kind though it be kept on the fire all day." (90).

This was somewhat similar to the account he gave of Tobar Chiarain in Laimsiadar.

Tobar Chùisdein

The OS Original Name Book gave a lengthy account when the sappers visited on 30 April, 1876: "St Cowstan's Well. A spring of excellent water between Garrabost and the shore. The water gushes out beneath the bank with considerable force and falls into the sea. On the farm of Garrabost. In ancient times the well was held in great esteem. Tradition is that all manner of diseases used to be cured by placing the patient under the cliff where the water falls to the shore."

This was undoubtedly a sacred spot, with the church and the well close to one another, having a special place in the affection of the people.

Tobar na Claich Glais   NB 522533

This well is to be found on the moor south of Allt na Muilne in Garrabost. The well is marked by a stone. It was visited in order to get relief from stomach pain.

An Tràiseachadh   NB 4433

This well is at the north end of Sandwick. People used to hear pipe music coming from it and, according to legend, the fairies spirited away a girl who was on her way to the well.

Fuaran Shòbhal   NB 348247

This well is above the road, north of Soval Lodge. This is a lively spring with a bottom of blue clay. The water is particularly cold, and would seem to contain sulphur.

Travellers often visited it. Fortunately, one Finlay Maciver looks after it, cleaning and caring for it: it is a pity there are not more like him to take an interest in these sites.

Fuaran an Dèididh   NB 415171

This well can be found in Calbost but only the name remains in people's memories. It is situated near the Tobar Mhòr. Another name for it was 'Fuaran a' Chapaill'. It has been filled to the top with stones for some unknown reason.

Fuaran an Dèididh   NB 3915

This well is at Loch Fuaran an Dèididh in Grabhair. According to Murdo Matheson from Grabhair, people visited this well when they suffered particularly severe toothache.

HARRIS

Tobraichean Uamh Uladal NB 078132

It is Martin Martin who has the first complete description of these two wells, which are in a cave high up in the side of Gleann Uladal. He says: "The largest and best fortified (cave), by nature, is that in the hill Ulweal, in the middle of a high rock; the passage leading to it is so narrow, that only one can enter at a time... The cave is capacious enough for 50 men to lodge in: it hath two wells in it, one of which is excluded from dogs; for they say if a dog do but taste of the water, the well presently drieth up: and for this reason, all such as have occasion to lodge there, take care to tie their dogs, that they may not have access to the water. The other well is called the dogs-well, and is only drunk by them." (112).

According to tradition a monster called Ula stayed in this cave, until it was killed by Dos Mòr Mac a' Cheannaiche. Dos' Stone, under which they are both said to be buried, is at the head of Loch Resort.

Tobar na Slàinte NB 1809

It is said that this well is situated up on the old Cliseam road. Nobody nowadays is sure of the exact location.

Tobar Mhàraig

Martin Martin describes this well: "There is one remarkable fountain lately discovered near Marvag-houses, on the eastern coast, and has a large stone by it, which is sufficient to direct a stranger to it. The natives find by experience that it is very effectual for restoring lost appetite; all that drink of it become very soon hungry, though they ate plentifully but an hour before: the truth of this was confirmed to me by those that were perfectly well, and also by those that were infirm; for it had the same effect on both." (112-112).

Tobar Amhainn Suidhe NB 0804

This is a small well, situated above the road at the west end of Amhainn Suidhe. Apparently the water was good for people; they saw it as a mineral well, with water similar to the well at Strathpeffer.

An Tobar Ruadh

An Tobar Ruadh

NF 020939

This well is situated at the north end of the burn close to a standing stone in the village of Borve.

It was said that water from this well would give a good appetite to those who drank from it and that the water had both health and curative qualities.

Martin Martin says of it: "There is a well in the heath, a mile east from the village of Borve; the natives say that they find it efficacious against colic, stitches, and gravel." (112).

Tobar Chè

NG 031992

This well is to be found on Taransay, close to Teampall Chè.

Tobar a' Ghobha

NG 134916

This well is on a croft at Leacan Lì. The water was used to relieve stomach cramp or headaches. It was said that An Gobha took water for the curing of illness from there either at dawn or at dusk; it is believed that An Gobha refers to the bard, Gobha na Hearadh.

Tobar Chuidinis

NG 8709

This well is among the crofts at Cuidinis (Croft No 6). The water in this well was used to perpetuate good health; Dr MacNab from Leverburgh used to take bottles of water from it to give those who were ill.

Tobar na Slàinte NG 021866

This well was in Leverburgh, across the bridge, on the south side of the road. It was good for restoring people's health. A high tide could fill it up but it would be clean again in three days' time.

Tobar na h-Annaid NF 975846

This well is on Cillegraigh, close to the cemetery, above Caolas Sgàire between the island and Easaigh.

The site of Teampall na h-Annaid is nearby; 'annaid' denotes the site of an ancient church. The name occurs elsewhere in the Western Isles: in Suainebost, in Siadar a' Chladaich and in the Shiants.

NORTH UIST

Tobar Leathad Ularaigh

This well is on the island of Berneray and close to Sgorr na Gruagaich. People believed that the gruagach or brownie liked to be close to water. The water from this well was considered to be the best on the Island.

Tobar Chaluim Chille   NF 873765

This one is up by Port nan Long south of Clachan. Beveridge (1900) says: "Fully half a mile to the south is an old well, now disused but still bearing the title of Tobar Chaluim Chille." (278). It tends to fill up with soil but every so often it is cleaned out.

Tobar Crò Naomh

This well was in Sanday. Carmichael (1900) says: "This one cannot be located, the extensive and once populous district being now almost uninhabited." (260).

Tobar Chaluim Chille

Tobar nan Sagart/Tobar nan Cupan

NF 838787

This well is close to the graveyard at Aird a' Mhorain, and to the cross in the rock. Pochin Mould (1953) says: "Nearby (to the cross) there is said to be a well called the Well of the Priest or the Well of the Cups, but I did not satisfactorily identify it, though there certainly were several small springs close to the cross. The cups refer to a cup-marked stone." (140-141). The Stornoway Gazette (11/1/77) says: "The cross is 200 yards west of the burial ground. Some yards to the south east of the cross a holy well overflows onto the shingly beach. Local names for it are 'well of the priest' and 'well of the cross'.

Tobar Bhàlaigh

This one was in Pàirc nan Each. It was said that the water in this well had similar qualities to the water in the spa at Strathpeffer.

Tobar Mheithinis

NF 712732

This well is situated by the shore out at Rubha Mheithinis, west of Baile Loch. It was known as a healing well. A lady from the area has a vague recollection that her brother on his death-bed requested a drink from this well.

Tobar Chuidhearaidh NF 809695

This well is situated to the east of Rathad na Comataidh on the south slope of Maireabhal.

People came to this well for a toothache cure, and they did not speak on the way there, until they had had a drink from the well. They would leave a gift or a coin and then they would kneel and recite the following verse:

Tha mise a' fàgail dèideadh
Lèireadh gus cnàimh mo chinn
Anns an tobair nach tràigh a chaoidh,
An ainm an Athar, A' Mhic 's an Spiorad Naoimh.

I hereby leave the toothache
Pain almost wasting my head
In the well that will never dry,
In the name of the Father, The Son and the Holy Ghost.

Carmichael (1900) refers to it as 'Tobar Chuidhairidh', Tobar an Dèididh', 'Tobar na cnoidh', (well of the worm) and 'Tobar cnuimh fhiacail' (well of the tooth worm', from a belief that toothache is caused by a worm in the tooth) (2, 11).

Tobar Chuidhearaidh

Tobar na Trianaid NF 815602

This well is approximately a quarter of a mile south west of Teampall na Trianaid in Càirinis. Beveridge (1900) writes: "Two hundred and fifty yards south-west of the twin chapels (Teampall na Trianaid and Teampall Clann Mhic a' Phiocair) is Tobar na Trianaid which in all probability served as the well in connection with them. This is lined with a wall, and although but recently disused is very shallow and of distinctly uninviting appearance." (288).

The OS Name Book says: "This name signifies The Trinity Well and is applied to the well situated about 12 chains to the South West of Teampall na Trianaid."

Alexander MacDonald from Càirinis used to say that people from South Uist came to this well on the day of Trinity, up to the 1840s. Somebody filled in the well since then: some of his sheep were being drowned there.

Tobar an Leighis NF 816603

This well was in Càirinis, north of Teampall na Trianaid and closer to the shore than to Cnoc na Trianaid. The well is now choked up with yellow iris.

BENBECULA

Tobar an Dèididh   NF 873765

This well is situated close to Teampull Chaluim Chille. Close to it is a cairn of stones and each person who visited the well seeking a remedy for toothache placed a stone on the cairn.

An Gamhnach   NF 826529

This well is out by the roadside, to the south east of Ruaidheabhal, opposite Loch Hearamal. People visited it and drank from it to improve their health; they brought a sprig of heather with them and left it at the well as an offering. Foxgloves grow round about the site.

Swire (1966) wrote: "But after his many days at sea St Torranan was very thirsty: finding no fresh water, he prayed to God for a spring and one at once broke out of the hillside where he stood. Torranan blessed it and when he had drunk his 'seven satisfactions' of its sweet water he gave it thanks and called the spring 'Gamhnach', Farrow Cow, and prayed that it might never dry up. Later, it became a place of pilgrimage and every pilgrim, having drunk, placed a 'choice green leaf' in it as thanks to the cow." (107).

An Gamhnach

SOUTH UIST

Tobar Ard a' Mhachair

This one was at Cròic, at the new graveyard. Bottles of water used to be taken from this well for medicinal purposes. It is said that this well disappeared under sand drift.

Tobar Crò Naomh

This well was in Druim Mòr. Carmichael (1900) refers to it: "A well at Drimore, in South Uist, is called 'Tobar Crò Naomh', Well of the Holy Heart. All who drank of its refreshing and curative waters placed a votive offering in the cairn beside the well." (260).

Tobar Beinn Ghòit

The well in Uisnis is situated between Beinn Ghòit and Beann a Tuath, about a mile from the lighthouse. It was visited for health purposes, and money used to be left in it.

Tobar Easbaig Eòghainn NF 804402

This well is out on the moor at the foot of Beinn an Tairbeirt. It was a health spring. Easbaig Eòghainn used to rest here, and have a drink from the well. It is well-built with stone walls.

Tobar Aonghais Ruaidh

This well is between Corodal and Hecla. The inhabitants of Dramasdal used to go to it, and they used to place pennies in it.

Tobar Creag an Fhìon

This well is very close to Uamh a' Phrionnsa. Bonnie Prince Charlie drank from this well and praised its water, and called it Tobar Creag an Fhìon – and the name continued. Clear water was said to be a form of wine; Duncan Bàn MacIntyre mentioned "fìon Allt na h-Annaid," or "wine from the stream of Annaid."

This is the well which the Ordnance Survey calls Tobar a' Phrionnsa: "This name given to a spring well of very pure water, which lies at the northern base of Beinn Sgreadhan. The name arose from Prince Charles visiting it when on the island. It means Prince's Well."

Tobar Aird Mhaoil
NF 718299

It was said that people drank out of this well when they were feeling unwell. It is situated on the northern shore of the headland. High tides fill it with stones and sand.

Tobar an Dèididh
NF 7534

This well is in the village of Snaoiseabhal, and the local people still know of it.

Tobar an Donnain
NF 730278

This one is in Cill Donnain on the croft belonging to Iain Dòmhnaill 'Ic Iain, close to the site of Teampall Chill Donnain (NF 731282). People used to take water from this well 'for illness'. It is well-built and has a wooden lid, and the water was used as sacred water.

Tobar Thiobartain
NF 7415

"Tobar Thiobartain nam buadh,
I air iomall an Domhain Mhòir."

(Tiobartan Well of the virtues, On the verge of the Great Domain).

This famous well was in Smercleit, 'seachd imrichean o rathad an rìgh'. According to tradition it was seven strips of land to the east of the road which goes along by the shore: nowadays it has disappeared into the machair land. Tiobar or tiobart means a well. So here we have the well of wells.

It was said locally that an old woman came to the well with a horse which had a squint, in order to cleanse the horse's eye with water from the well. Because of this the well lost its powers. It closed up from then onwards. Carmichael (1900) gives a good account:

"Tobar Thiobartan nam buadh
A chasgas gach falc is fual.
An eilean iomartach a' chuain
Am fìor iomall an domhainn mhòir."

"The well of Tiobartan of virtues
To quell flood and gravel,
In remotest isle of the ocean,
On the very verge of the great domain."

According to tradition, the well of Tiobartan was famous in olden times, the pilgrims resorting to it from afar. Then a man brought his sick horse to it, and the spirit of the well fled, shrieking, and never returned. The well is in the machair, near the sea, and is now filled with drift sand. (286).

Tobar Adhratobhta NF 796200

This well is close to Cill Choinnich, north east of Loch Baghasdal. The stones from the church were used to make the sheep-fank and the fank is on the site of the church. The well itself is situated amongst whins. Oral tradition has it that fishermen visited the well on their way to and from fishing.

Tobar na Reulaig NF 783096

This well is on Eriskay. It is a fist-sized hole in a stone slab between Uamh na Lice Ruaidhe and Sloc Ruadh, west of Reulaig. The hole is eight inches deep and can hold a pint of rain water. Local fishermen used it regularly.

BARRA

Tobar nan Ceann

Tradition has it that a battle was fought on the island of Fuideigh and that three soldiers or Norsemen were beheaded; their heads were thrown into this well.

It was from Nan MacKinnon of Vatersay that I first heard tales which made reference to human heads in connection with wells. Although she began by telling of Fuideigh and the Norsemen, she would always come back to Mòr nan Ceann. In these tales she would make reference to Tobar nan Ceann, Tobar a' Chinn and Tobar Mòr nan Ceann, but she did not know the exact whereabouts of the well itself.

She told one tale which said that Lady MacNeil was herself Mòr nan Ceann and that she is buried on Eilean Bhuneasain beside Caibeal Moire nan Ceann or Cill Bhrianain. According to her, Mòr nan Ceann ordered three men to be beheaded, and she washed the heads in Tobar Bharra before they were buried and that Mòr's own son, Ruairidh, was made chief of the clan.

But there existed different 'versions' (as she herself would say) of this tale: some of them very strange and complicated (see Ross, 1961, 1962). In each tale a well has pride of place, and three heads in a creel, and a head which spoke, and a head or heads which are placed in a well. It is certain that what we have here is part of ancient oral tradition, with wells and human heads in close association.

Tobar a' Dhùgain   NF 6702

This well is in Bealach a' Dhùgain past Dubharaidh at Baile na Creige, and across from a' Chrìochain. The well was blessed by Father Dermont Duggan, so that the Barra people could drink from it and have support and intercession from him.

Dermont Duggan was sent to Barra by St Vincent de Paul in 1650, as the people had been without a priest for nearly eighty years.

(The Reformation had taken place in 1560).

Tobar Bharra   NF 706075

This is one of the most famous wells in the Western Isles. It is situated near Cille Bharra, on the east side of the road. It is a lovely well with a sandy bottom and an attractive appearance with the water bursting forth in three springs. The well is steeped in tradition. It was said that it was St Barr himself who opened the well; that he put his stick three times into the ground and that the three springs arose, none of them having dried up from that day forth.

Tobar Bharra

Tobar air Beinn Eòlagaraidh   NF 702074

There is a well close to the top of Beinn Eòlagaraidh, and although its name is not known, it is the subject of a particular tradition, accounts of which have appeared in many history books as far back as the 1660s. This is called the tale of the cockles.

Boece's history of 1527 gives an account of cockles having been in a well in Mull. But it was not long until the tale appeared on Barra.

Of the early accounts, it is Dean Munro's account of 1594 which is the best known: "In the north end of this Countrey of Barray there is ane heich know. Upon the heid of this know thair is ane spring and fresh water well. This well trewlie springis up certane lile round quhyte things... likst to the shape, figure and form on ame little Cockle as it apperit to me." (73-74).

Another account, round about the same time (in MacFarlane, 1630) puts it thus: "Ther is one litle spring and fresh water running out of ane grein hill above the Church, which doeth flow into the sea. And there are springand there certane litill Cockles shells which they alleadge that the samen doth flow into the sea out of the Well and doeth grow in another place next the Church not the tenth part of ane myll from the Church of Barray called Killbarray." The story becomes a bit difficult to follow.

Some of the accounts place the well on the plain – maybe Tobar Bharra, as we know it. For example, an earlier account in 1600 in Skene states: "Item, in this Ile (Barraigh) is ane weill quhairin growis cockles, quihilk is at the fute of ane hill callit the Hill of Barra, twa mile fra the sea." Martin Martin himself visited Barra and went to Tobar Bharra: "And they say that the Well of Kilbar throws up embryoes of cockles, but I did not discern any in the rivulet, the air being at that time foggy." (158). Did he by any chance refer to the wrong well!

The tale was still told in the 20th century. Alasdair Alpin MacGregor (1929) was of the opinion that he had secured the answer: "The spring which is identified locally as being the one that threw up 'embryoes of cockles' is situated within three or four yards of the summit of Ben Eoligarry. The water in it is charged with calcium carbonate, which is deposited on sand grains and similar objects, thus giving rise to the superstition that the water contained minute cockles." (276).

And MacGregor (1929) also says: "Apart from the Well of Kilbar, whence the cockles found in such immense quantities on the Tràigh Mhòr were supposed to have been carried down, the well of St Mary and the well of St Barr are the only sources of fresh water in this vicinity." (316). So, is Tobar Chille Bharra the one on Beinn Eòlagaraidh and is St Barr's well the one with the sandy grain deposits? But where is Tobar Mhoire, Well of St Mary, in this locality?

And there is another story about another well round about here, but there is no certainty as to which one. There is an account in MacFarlane (1630) which tells of an incident of which the MacNeil of Barra and an old man told and in which they believed: "There is also a spring of fresh water... When appearance of wars were to be in the the Countrey of Barray that certaine drops of blood hath oftymes bein sein in this spring and fresh Water Well. Lykewise whenever appearance of peace wold be in the Countrie that certain little bits of Peitts would be seen."

Between the cockles and the blood, the tales which are told about the wells around Cille Bharra are as interesting as any that are told about wells anywhere.

Tobar Cùl Beinn na h-Oib   NF 6902

This is a healing well, in the Dark Glen. People visited the well for health reasons. A lady from Buaile nam Bodach told of how a local man kept going to the well for healing purposes for as long as he could.

It can be seen on the OS map as 'mineral well'.

The road to it runs alongside Loch an Dùin, and it is about 500 yards from the main road; about 10 steps away on the south side of the road.

Tobar Chaluim Chille   NF 649996

This well is in Tangasdal near Loch Thangasdal, in a place called A' Bheirbh. This is a particularly attractive well, large with sandy surrounds: the water is particularly hard.

This is both a blessing and wishing well. Nan MacKinnon (Nan Eachainn Fhionnlaigh) from Vatersay recounted that if you required anything all you had to do was to go there and make a wish which would be fulfilled. People visited the well in order to receive a blessing, particularly before embarking on a journey – such as the herring girls. They came to it the Sunday before they left. Also couples who intended to marry but could not afford to until the next season, came to it: they would come to the well on Sunday to make a vow of fidelity.

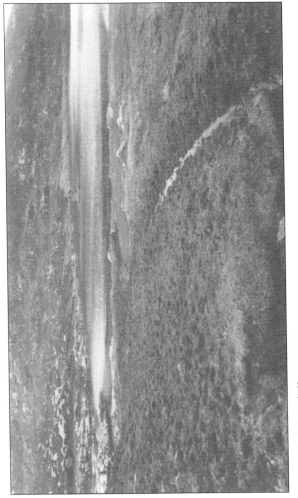

Tobar Chaluim Chille

In past times when a lot of fisherman were coming into Barra, Brethren fishermen from Buckie came to the well every Sunday. The Barra fishermen themselves went there every Sunday to drink from it, in the hope of getting a better catch during the week. Martin Martin (1696) says: "There is another well not far from Tangstill, which the inhabitants say in a fertile year throws up many grains of barley in July and August." (157).

Tobar nam Buadh   NF 665979

This well is situated in the forecourt of Caisteal Chiosmul in Castlebay. It is highly unusual for a well to be situated on a sea rock, and this has meant that the castle has been a particularly good fortress. The water in this well was noted for having healing qualities for smallpox.

Tobar Chaluim Chille   NL 565833

This well is in Mingulay. It is close to Cill Chaluim Chille, with the water coming out of the rock. Nan MacKinnon (Nan Eachainn Fhionnlaigh) from Vatersay had this information.

Tobar Chaluim Chille

Tradition has it that this one was situated on Ceann Bharraigh, but there is no evidence of it now.

ST. KILDA

Tobar nam Buadh   NA 088003

This well is particularly noteworthy in the history of St. Kilda because definite practices and oral tradition are connected with it. Martin Martin wrote: "In this isle there are plenty of excellent fountains or springs; that near the female warrior's house is reputed to be the best, the name of it, Toubir-nim-buey, importing no less than the well of qualities or virtues; it runneth from east to west, being sixty paces ascent above the sea: I drank of it twice, an English quart at each time; it is very clear, exceedingly cold, light, and diuretick; I was not able to hold my hands in it for above a few minutes, in regard of its coldness; the inhabitants of Harries find it effectual against windy-chollicks, gravel, head-aches; this well has a cover of stone." (414).

TS Muir depicts it as: "A low square-shaped massy stone building, with a stone roof, covers the spring, which, after forming a pool in the floor of the cell, runs down the russet slope like a thread of silver to join the stream in the valley." (65).

MacAulay (1764) tells of how the people gave pride of place to the well and of how they believed in its properties: 'Some little time ago, a person long afflicted with a distemper, which had defeated the skill of all the people about him, took it in his head to go from Harris to St. Kilda, upon a sort of religious pilgrimage. His meaning was, to lay his grievance before the patron of this foundation." (94). Strangely no account is given as to whether this person achieved any satisfaction on account of the trip to the well.

But his account is nonetheless helpful: "It was once a fundamental article of faith in this isle, that the water here was a sovereign cure for a great variety of distempers, deafness particularly, and every nervous disease. Near the fountain stood an altar, on which the distressed votaries laid down their oblations. Before they could touch the sacred water, with any prospect of success, it was their constant practice to address the Genius of the place with supplication and prayer. No one approached him with empty hands. But the devotees were abundantly frugal: the offerings presented by them were the poorest acknowledgements that could be made to a superior Being, from whom they had either hopes or fears. Shells and pebbles, rags of linen or stuffs worn out, pins, needles, or rusty nails, were generally all the tribute that was paid; and sometimes, though rarely enough, copper coins of the smallest value. Very frequently the whole expense of sacrifice was no more than some one of the little common stones that happened to be in the Pilgrim's way." (95-96). Beside the well there is a stone which was used as an altar, and it was there that they left their offerings.

MacAulay concludes: "The Saint, Angel, or Deity, to whom the wonder working Tobernimbuadh pertained, is now an unknown Being, his name having been long ago buried in oblivion." (100-101).

As I stood day after day drinking from the clear water of Tobar nam Buadh in Gleann Mòr, close to the house of the Ban-àrmainn, I could not help but think of the many people who came there to drink, now without trace, and the writings which have given us such insight into the lives of these people.

Tobar a' Chlèirich

MacAulay (1764) says: "The second holy well at St. Kilda is below the village, and gushes out like a torrent from the face of a rock. At every full tide the sea overflows it, but how soon that ebbs away, nothing can be fresher or sweeter that the water. The natives call it Toberi Clerich." (99).

Tobar Childa

Much has also been written about this well, because many were of the opinion that it carried the same name as did the island itself. Martin wrote: "There is a large well near the town, called St. Kilder's Well; from which the island is supposed to derive its name; this water is not inferior to that above-mentioned (Tobar nam Buadh); it runneth to the south-east from the north-west." (414).

MacAulay (1764) wrote: "The third sacred fountain at St. Kilda is near the heart of the village, and is of universal use in the community. The water of it is sweet, light and clear like crystal. The people give it the name of tobar Childa Chalda." It is thought by some that that the word 'childa' stems from the Norse word 'kelda' meaning 'a well'.

Tobar na Cille   NA 098984

This well is beside the site of Teampall Bhrianain, close to Geodha Chille Bhrianain. According to oral tradition if the wind was not favourable for fishing, the fishermen would go to Tobar na Cille and each of them would stand astride the well for an instant, as a result of which the wind would become favourable.

Tobar na h-Oige

It was said that this well is situated in the face of a rock. Martin spoke of it thus: "There is a celebrated well issuing out of the face of a rock on the north-side of the east bay, called by the inhabitants and others, The Well of Youth, but is only accessible to the inhabitants, no stranger daring to climb the steep rock; the water of it is received as it falls, into the sea; it runs towards the south-east." (414). Although this well described by Martin is no longer to be seen, oral tradition tells of another well by the same name which appeared in another part of the island. One day a man, tired as could be, was descending Conochair with a sheep on a lead. He came upon a spring which he had never seen before. He drank from it and felt as young as a youth. He left the sheep at that spot, and ran down to the village to tell about the well.

When he returned, there was no sign of sheep or well. It was said that if he had left a piece of iron at the well that neither the well nor the sheep would have disappeared. As happens naturally, the well of youth had evaded him!

Other wells are mentioned as being situated on St. Kilda, although we have little information about them. One of these was Tobar Chonasdain, and Martin wrote about that one: "There is another well half a mile of this (St. Kilder's Well), nam'd after one Conirdan, an hundred paces above the sea, and runneth from north-west towards the south-east, having a stone cover." (414). There is also mention of Tobar a' Mhinisteir, but the name itself is all that remains.

BIBLIOGRAPHY

M. MacLeod Banks, 1937, British Calendar Customs: Scotland. Vol 1. William Glaisher for the Folk-lore Society.

George F. Black, 1893, Scottish Charms and Amulets, PSAAS, 3, 433-526.

Alexander Carmichael, 1972, Carmina Gadelica. Scottish Academic Press.

Alexander Fraser, 1878(a), Ancient Wells in the North and Their Folk-Lore, Inverness Scientific Society & Field Club. Vol 1, 119-146; 1878(b) Northern Folk-Lore on Wells and Water, The Celtic Review, 3, 348-460.

Kenneth MacAulay, 1764, The History of St. Kilda. James Thin.

A. M. MacFarlane, 1927, Myths Associated with Mountains, Springs, and Lochs in the Highlands, TGSI, 34, 131-152.

Alasdair Alpin MacGregor, 1925, Behold the Hebrides! W&R Chambers; 1929, Summer Days Among the Western Isles. Nelson.

Alexander MacGregor, 1922, Highland Superstitions. Eneas MacKay.

James M. MacKinlay, 1893, Folklore of Scottish Lochs and Springs. William Hodge.

Finlay MacLeod, 1997, The Chapels in the Western Isles. Acair.

F. Marian McNeill, 1957, The Silver Bough: Scottish Folklore and Folk-belief. Vol 1. William MacLennan.

Malcolm MacPhail, 1898, Articles on Lewis Chapels. Oban Times.

Martin Martin, 1934, A Voyage to St. Kilda; A Description of the Western Isles of Scotland. Eneas Mackay.

Arthur Mitchell, 1862, On Various Superstitions in the North-West Highlands and Islands of Scotland, Especially in Relation to Lunacy, PSAS, 4, 251-288, 1880, The Past in the Present. David Douglas.

Dean Monro, 1549, Western Isles of Scotland. (ed. R. W. Munro, 1961, Oliver and Boyd).

T. S. Muir, 1861, Characteristics of Old Church Architecture; 1885, Ecclesiological Notes on Some of the Islands of Scotland. David Douglas.

Thomas Pennant, 1774, A Tour in Scotland, and Voyages to the Hebrides; 1772. Chester.

Anne Ross, 1961, A Story from Vatersay, Scottish Studies, 5, 108-109; 1962, Severed Heads in Wells: an Aspect of Well Cult, Scottish Studies, 31-48; 1976, The Folklore of the Scottish Highlands. B. T. Batsford.

Royal Commission, 1928, Ancient and Historical Monuments of Scotland: The Outer Hebrides, Skye and the Small Isles. HMSO.

Otta S. Swire, 1966, The Outer Hebrides and their Legends. Oliver and Boyd.

J. Russell Walker, 1883, "Holy Wells" in Scotland, PSAS, 152-210.

NOTES

NOTES